Tie My Shoes

Rising above My Disability

LONNIE E. SHIPE

Tie My Shoes
Rising above My Disability

iUniverse books may be ordered through booksellers or by contacting:

iUniverse
1663 Liberty Drive
Bloomington, IN 47403
www.iuniverse.com
1-800-Authors (1-800-288-4677)

ISBN: 978-1-5320-8517-8 (sc)
ISBN: 978-1-5320-8518-5 (e)

Library of Congress Control Number: 2019915878

Print information available on the last page.

iUniverse rev. date: 10/09/2019

This book is dedicated in Loving Memory to my Mother Ruth Shipe

Who gave me birth and raised me.

To my beautiful and loving wife Eugenia.

To my beautiful daughter Alexis who I love dearly.

To my grandchildren

Ashton and Ace

All the people that help support me through school, college and through life itself. And to my friend Dr.

Leo Provost, Retired U.S. Army

For his encouragement to keep writing.

Can't Never Did Anything

With the love of Jesus, family, friends, counseling and a belief
deep inside my heart, it is my burning passion to share my journey to
help someone have a better life for themselves.

Names and have been changed.

My Preface:

"Tie My Shoes", is a story about Lonnie E. Shipe, my life. Born premature with cerebral palsy, living and functioning in a normal society while attending a public school system. Battling the struggles with leg braces, crutches and a "funny voice" and trying to be "normal" when my body, was far from normal.

Some educators and medical doctors had little hope of me succeeding through school. As one medical doctor stated, when I was in the ninth grade, "This will be Lonnie's last year of school, C. P.'ers only go to the ninth grade."

With my dreams, hope, faith in God and the attitude my mother gave me in my childhood, "Can't never did anything, try and try again," And working hard against the odds of physical barriers, the educational system and others for nearly a decade, to earn my Associate Degree, Bachelors Degree and a Masters Degree in Counseling Education, with a post Graduate School Internship in Counseling Education.

Then adding to this struggle, "to just belong" I fell off my crutches and broke my neck. Life seemed to be ten times more difficult, in a millisecond.

The struggles of dating, sexuality, self-worth, depression, suicidal thoughts, to a wonderful marriage, a beautiful daughter and two grandsons. All of this because my mother kept repeating, "try and try again."

With my desire to help inspire someone, sometime, somewhere, somehow, hopefully my writing will do so.

Sincerely,

Lonnie E. Shipe

Contents

Tying My Shoes

Tying a shoelace, it is so simple. It only takes a few easy, quick seconds to tie a shoe lace. A blind person can tie a shoelace. But explain to someone with Cerebral Palsy or Parkinson disease, how easy it is to tie a shoelace or carry a cup of liquid without dropping or spilling the liquid.

Here I will share my personal thoughts on life and how people helped me along my way. This motivation, attempting to share these thoughts, is to inspire other people to, "Never Give Up."

The roads we travel may not be easy, but our legacy is formed with each passing day. In every decision or actions we make daily, will be watched and remembered by people around us, especially Jesus.

These thoughts will attempt to 'show" the real world, the generalization of people cannot always be generalized. We need to stand up as individuals, and do well for each other and God.

Jesus was my greatest power before I even knew him. The plan was to keep me alive, all three pounds and three ounces at birth. Doctors did not expect me to live but there was hope, if I kept on living. Jesus kept me alive after coming close to death as a new born and at other times in my life. Jesus always has a plan.

Mother was my second greatest power. She worked with me on doing my daily exercises, practicing my writing, breathing, talking and molded me into the person that I am today. She never gave up on me.

"Can't never did anything," was a phrase mother told me hundreds of times while growing up.

Cerebral Palsy or C.P. was a major handicap to live and deal with. But the spinal cord injury from my bathroom fall when I was forty-two, is the most difficult situation for me. As a young person I often asked God, "Why me?" While struggling with my daily living, absolutely nothing was easy, I just could not understand why, but God knew.

"Mom I am so lucky," I said while looking at other children in twisted bodies in numerous types of strollers or wheelchairs at the C.P. Clinic. Awkwardly, I moved with crutches and leg braces from my waist to my ankles.

Leaning against objects was the only way to set up by myself as an infant and to this day. My limited mobility consisted of being carried by someone or by crawling on the floor, until around the age of five.

"Hey mom, can you hear me?" I screamed in my distorted speech from the top of my lungs. The radio was turned up full volume, while she was in another room doing other things to make me yell louder.

"Did you call me?" she asked, "yell louder." Many times I thought if she only, "turned down the radio a little she could hear me." Yelling or even talking was difficult work for me. Yelling and crying was necessary for me to breathe deeply. And therapeutic spankings were necessary to breathe correctly or I would stop breathing.

There is no doubt that my parents did everything safely and humanely possible so they could to keep me living.

Even today as a senior citizen I am unable to blow bubbles with bubble gum. A personal medical doctor was very concerned with my breathing and pneumonia.

She suggested I use a plastic jug, put in some dish soap and filled up the jug nearly full of water and blow bubbles into the jug with a straw. After all what did anyone expect of my lungs when I was never able to run to expand my lungs.

Holding my head up, straight and steady was always difficult to see where I was going. The droopy head symptom developed because of my weak neck muscles from infancy to elementary school age.

For an exercise, mother placed books on my head to balance the books and learn to hold my head up. Then in high school, my neck size was sixteen and one half inches from using crutches for thirteen years. But my body weight was maybe one hundred pounds. Often I used my neck to hold my body steady on furniture while getting up off the floor.

As a young child, I never had a wheelchair other than baby strollers. My parents carried me everywhere. Or I crawled on my hands and knees until the age of five and I never talked until five also. My first wheelchair was after my first surgery on my legs in the fourth grade, during those recovery months.

Another symptom I had in my early life was drooling. And I have been told, "You talk funny."

Mother encouraged me to keep trying new things, to perhaps keep me out of a nursing home in my adult life.

"I can't mom. I can't do this," I would say growing frustrated and angry by the second at my stupid body.

"Can't never did anything," she always informed me.

"At first, if you don't succeed. Try and try again," I think I heard those phrases from mother a million times growing up. Thank you Jesus, mother was never a quitter, she never gave up on me.

It was not a joyful experience doing these painful, stupid exercises. Other normal children did not need to do these, being normal was not me.

Chewing gum was an enjoyable exercise that taught me how to swallow food, my saliva and stop continuously drooling, another Cerebral Palsy symptom.

Learning to control my tongue, lips, jaws and throat helped with my speech. The association of exercise at the time, meant muscle pain and crying.

The turmoil, mental anger and stress of not having the ability to communicate our thoughts, ideas or desire would be totally overwhelming for me.

My legs were skinny and bony but not as badly as many CP (cerebral palsy), children's legs were.

The little girl not far from me, one afternoon at the C. P. Clinic sat in her baby stroller drooling. We were both maybe six years old. She was pretty with her brown hair and nice dress but her body twitched uncontrollably.

And I wanted to talk with her, give her some attention and help her to feel a little better.

She looked at me trying to smile with her spastic, twisted facial muscles. Her body twitched even more uncontrollably, which were much worse than my spasms. My thoughts of this little girl in her condition confused my mind into helplessness.

There were probably many times in my life, when some people never approached me because they did not know what to do or say around me. Some people could not understand what I was saying or maybe they did not feel comfortable with me.

My legs were also twisted, skinny, crooked and bony. Yet I felt "so lucky" and blessed, I could still move around and play in my own way.

Being around other disabled children just made me see myself through them, disabled. Normal children I wanted to be around, so maybe I could be more like normal children.

Fighting this war within myself, to just be normal over the years somehow got twisted in my brain and developed into self-hate.

And a body that functioned normally was my childhood daily prayer. God never answered that prayer in the way I wanted. As a child, I sometimes thought I was a bad person because God was not answering my prayers, perhaps I was too young to understand.

But most of all, I just wanted to be in a normal person's world with a body like my best boyhood friend, I will not use his real names. But my friend knows who I am writing about. He was blessed with an athletic type of body. To me everything came so easily, skillfully, fluidly and gracefully for him. My dreams and prayer were to be just like my best friend.

My speech was strained at my young age. Other words to describe my physical and emotional being was, "funny, crooked legs, goofy speech or different," anything, but a cripple. And I was one of them, a "cripple." It was never a good feeling for me to hear that word, I hated that word. For me 'cripple," just describes things as useless or not good. Being handicapped sounded better to me.

Myself, I felt so lucky; I could at least stand up, not by myself of course, because I did not have a sense of balance. There was always something needed or someone for me to hold onto or someone holding onto me before I could stand up. Nor would I, in my lifetime have the ability to stand by myself.

Standing Table and Walking Bars

About the age of five, I learned to use leg braces and crutches for walking. The heavy waist high leg braces were made of leather straps, buckles and leather pads covering my calves, thighs and knees with steel bars on both sides of each leg and brace shoes.

Around my back and waist was a steel band covered in leather that was shaped and designed with a leather strap to buckle around my stomach.

With the aid of the crutches and braces I was able to stand up and walk around for the first time without another person's assistance or a physical object for assistance, such as a chair, couch or bed. The heavy, stiff black leather high top shoes were laced up like boots. Then my shoes were clamped into my heavy leg braces.

The tight, stiff muscles in my legs would not allow me to pick up my crooked pigeon toed feet up and off of the floor, when I took my steps.

Walking is not a correct word for me to use to describe my ambulatory motion, in my view, it was more like jostling, because I am not really walking.

My best friend's family and my family, as a young boy were good friends. Our dad's had the imagination and initiative to build and repair things for me.

One summer day, when I was maybe four years old, my friend's dad and my dad worked very hard together lifting and lugging in a big heavy bright red wooden "standing table," up the three stone and cement steps onto the old farm house front porch.

Often I crawled down or fell down, scraping my hands, fingers, knees and sometimes my head on the hard, on those cool rough cement steps, to play in the front yard, before I had my crutches or braces.

The big bright red table banged heavily on the cement porch floor. Both men let out a sigh of relief from their effort and wiped their forehead of sweat from the hard work of moving the heavy "standing table."

This table was built with a swinging and latching wooden door. And I could stand up in this small wooden square box. The standing box fit closely around my body from my chest to the floor. With the hope that I could stand up without falling and play on the table, and strengthen my thin, weak, skinny, crooked legs and feet.

The outside edge around the tabletop had an inch or so border higher than the table top. This prevented my crayons, toys, marbles or any other plaything from rolling off the table onto the floor.

Slowly, I started to crawl on my hands and knees toward the table because I still could not walk or stand upright unassisted. Dad gently and easily picked me up off the cement porch and "stood" me in the red box, shut and latched the door shut to keep me "standing" there safely.

Happily, there I was standing for the very first time in my life without assistance from someone or gripping onto an object. There were no words could I use to explain my happiness, wonder and joy.

It did not take long for my skinny, crooked legs to get tired of standing. Over time, my standing up time increased.

The tendons behind my knees and ankles were extremely tight, like steel cables and they did not allow my knees or my ankles to bend, or be completely straight into a normal posture. My body was stupid I thought, because it never cooperated with my wishes.

The Achilles tendons behind the heels were so short, my feet were pigeon toed and I walked on my toes. The Adductor Magnus muscles in my groin, was so tight, the inside of my knees would rub together with each and every step.

All through grade school, up until my junior year in college I needed new pants every few months because the pants would wear a half-inch size hole in the pant legs at the inside knee joints.

Often the skin on the inside of my knee joints would be bleeding from both of the knees rubbing against each other with every step I took.

Along with the red standing table, dad and his friend made me some waking bars. These parallel walking bars were another piece of homemade equipment that I used to learn to walk with. The parallel bars were made of steel water pipes. The pipes were fitted like a rectangle with legs to stand about thirty inches high off the floor.

With the walking bars, I could grab onto the bars and jostle with my crooked legs, knot knees and pigeon toed, tip toed feet. But I could "walk" back and forth, just like a dog on a chain but it was a joy just to be "walking."

But I was trying to teach my body to walk. As always, my body never cooperated with my wishes. My younger sisters were walking and I was not, with this stupid body.

Overtime, I grew stronger then I could pick one end of the walking bars up off the front porch floor and slide the bars all around the front porch, I was finally learning to walk I thought.

My first wheelchair was homemade by my mother. She combined the baby carriage frame and wheels with a child's rocking chair without the rockers, to become a wheelchair or stroller. That was the only "wheelchair" I remember using from preschool to fourth grade.

My Friends Visiting Me at the Hospital

One afternoon while learning to walk with crutches and leg braces for the first time at the children hospital, I received a joyful, unexpected surprise from four hours' drive away. Two of my friends surprised me from back home, they walked into the big therapy room where I was "learning to walk."

My visitors were my parent's high school friends. Being a bit home sick from my three week hospital stay, it was a tremendous joy and I was so very happy to see them.

Two physical therapists were working with me, teaching me the correct walking techniques, while wearing my first leg braces and crutches. This was extremely difficult, painful and exhausting work for me. But it was fun, to learn my new way of getting around because, "I wanted to walk."

This room from previous visits had been a busy therapy room. Today this big, unused room filled with tables, children's crutches and medical equipment. The unlighted side of this room had dark shadows lurking around in the corners, a change of time.

My visitors were standing quietly observing me learning to walk for the very first time in my life at the age of five.

"OK Lonnie show your friends how you are learning to walk," one therapist said encouraging me.

"Lonnie has been doing so well," added the other therapist, as she glanced over at my friends while holding onto the therapy gait belt that was snugly around my waist to keep me from falling down.

This was so difficult moving these crooked, stiff, tight legs in these heavy leg braces strapped and buckled on my legs and waist. These heavy braces were guiding my legs into a walking motion in which my legs never went before, causing a powerful strong resistance with my legs and the leather and steel braces.

It was exciting and a good feeling to show my friends that I was learning to walk, but I was also scared too of falling down and embarrassing myself. As difficult, painful and slow as this walking was, I realized this had to be better than crawling on my hands and knees to get around.

"Remember', the therapist whispered quietly in my ear, "start out with your right crutch, then move your left foot. Then step with your left crutch and then step with your right foot," she added.

My head nodded, acknowledging her advice as I tightly gripped my crutches with my fingers. Looked down at my brown leather shoes on my feet wishing them to easily move but I knew this would be difficult, hard work for me.

Sucking in my breath deeply through my mouth and held the breath tightly within my lungs, while straining every muscle in my body. My feet did not move. Still stuck after all of my straining, it felt like my shoes were glued to the shiny tiled floor.

"You need to get going," I silently but sternly told my feet. Suddenly, my therapist rescued me, I felt her push gently on my safety gait belt that was around my waist, nudging my body forward into motion saving me from embarrassment.

With my straining muscles and exertion of physical effort, the right crutch moved forward a few inches. My body twisted and shifted sideways, then forward, back and forth my body slowly moved. My brain seemed to be screaming at my feet and legs to get moving.

My left foot and shoe drug slowly across the floor like a stiff, crooked, bent stick. My feet only moved just three or four inches with each step at a time.

Then suddenly, for an unknown reason my foot or crutch would shoot out uncontrollably into a larger step, causing me to flinch and lose my balance and embarrass myself in front of my friends. It was a secure feeling my two therapists were beside me, helping to support and keep me upright.

Everyone was extremely happy, smiling and applauding, to see me standing up for the first time and using the crutches and braces jostled across the room. Through all of this work, I was excited and happy over my accomplishments but I was very tired too. But I could not understand why this was so difficult.

Two other exercises I did at the clinic were breathing exercises. My first four, five or so years in my life I was not a very active child so my lungs never developed normally. And I had trouble breathing and I spoke not much louder than a whisper.

Often I heard, my mother tell the doctors and other people, "Lonnie never talked until he was five years old." Even today as an adult I have trouble breathing when anyone fries food, the aroma of the hot cooking oil is truly suffocating to me.

One exercise I did as a youngster was simply blowing soap bubbles. This caused me to blow with deeper breaths and longer periods, to create more bubbles and a longer bubble floating time. The purpose was to expanding my lungs to breathe better.

Another breathing exercise I enjoyed at the clinic was with a cerebral palsied boy about my age and our speech therapist, who sat between us and facing the same direction.

Then the therapist reached into a small box of toys and pulled out a small wooden red airplane.

"With this plane we are going to see how far this plane can fly. But this airplane will only fly if you two boys make a humming noise causing the airplane engines to keep running," she explained.

"And the louder you hum the faster the plane will go," she added. Both of us boys agreed to her plan and I was excited to play this breathing game.

The therapist gently set the airplane on my left knee holding the airplane in her fingertips. Sucking in quickly a deep gulp of air into my lungs to be sure the engines would not shut down causing the airplane to crash.

"Huummm" an audible sound came from my lips, as I easily hummed. The toy airplane slowly lifted off my left knee, across the therapist lap to the other boy's right knee where the toy airplane safety landed.

"That was very good Lonnie," she joyfully said to me. Thinking silently to myself, "that was not too hard to do. It was kind of fun too." The other boy returned the airplane back to my knee in a similar manner.

Back and forth the plane flew.

"That was good guys an excellent flight," as the therapist encouraged us.

"Your turn Lonnie, take a deep breath," she added.

Joyfully and eagerly I sucked in a deep breath through my mouth, feeling my chest expand. "Humm," I started my humming noise for the motor to keep running in our imaginations. The toy airplane took off the second time, from my left knee just like the previous trip across the therapist lap. This will be easy, I thought silently.

But suddenly, I watched the therapist turn the airplane into a circling route in mid-air, making it much harder work and to hum a little longer than the previous trip.

"Alright guys. Both of you are doing great with this airplane and the breathing exercises. But the afternoon is getting late. We have just enough time for one more flight. Are you two guys ready?" the speech therapists eagerly and joyfully asked.

Both of us boys shook our heads and excitedly yelled "yes." We are ready for one last flight.

"Take a deep breath Lonnie," she said as I sucked in another deep breath down into my lungs. My lungs were tightly expanding and felt very heavy and almost hurting, ready to burst I thought.

"Huummm," I loudly hummed, proud of my previous efforts. But the airplane took off much slower than the previous trips. Suddenly, I was worried that I would not have enough air in my lungs to make the airplane fly for the complete trip.

The therapist mention something about the airplane was fully loaded with cargo this time.

Then quickly my lungs started hurting. Squeezing my chest tightly I pushed out as much air as I could from my lungs. The three of us agreed in the beginning we could not let this airplane crash. But the airplane was only about half way to its destination and I was losing wind power from exhaling from my lungs.

Eagerly, we watched the therapist turn the airplane into a circling route in mid-air making it much harder work and to hum a little longer than the previous trip. "The flight pattern is the same, just a heavier cargo and head-wind," the therapist added smiling at us. This was not so easy after all I thought. But the airplane did land safely on the other boy's knee.

"Great job boys, but it is time to go to lunch, see you tomorrow", our therapist said, as I jostled up on my crutches feeling good about my performance.

When I Was Growing Up

When I was three or four years old, several times nightly I would wake up crying and screaming for my parents with terrible charlie horse cramps in my legs.

Mom or dad would hurriedly but sleepily come in my bedroom and massage and straighten my crooked legs, often by force by pushing my legs muscles as straight as possibly.

From this pain I would cry even more. For several minutes, my parents massaged and stretched my leg muscles, until my muscle cramps slowly subsided and I slowly drifted back to sleep.

Many nights I tried staying awake as long as I could, from worry and fear knowing the pain would return in my legs. Almost like a demon that only works in the silent, dark night and inflicting pain on my little, skinny, bony legs, stabbing my legs over and over with sharp knives.

This must have been a trying, difficult time for my parents because they did everything they possibly could with my pain. Followed the doctor's advice they were still helplessly watching my pain come back nightly, during my preschool years.

"Why did I have all this pain?" I asked mom many times. Her only answer would be, "I do not know Lonnie. God only knows. But we just have to keep working on this and other things."

But I was too young to realize what mother was saying to me. And nearly a life time later, I never thought much about her comment but she taught me, "God is in control. We somehow need to let His way be His way and keep working harder, do our best, to help ourselves and our fellow man."

Should Be Walking Before High School

The doctor's appointments were always routine on the semi-annual trips to the cerebral palsy clinic. And I remember listening to the many conversations between my mother and the doctors.

The doctor said, "Lonnie should be walking by the time he reaches high school." And I remember thinking at the time, "Oh that is happy, exciting news. When I get older I will be walking like my classmates and friends."

That never happened and years later I never understood why the doctor would say such a thing. When he probably knew, I would never walk without the aid of crutches or leg braces.

Then I wondered, was he giving me false hope to keep my dreams and motivation alive, deep in my heart, I do not know, but as a young boy, the doctor did give me hope.

In time, I was told cerebral palsy was brain damage and this led me to believe affected my movements, lack of balance and my "funny voice," and with something not "connecting correctly" with my brain.

At another hospital in Chicago a doctor glued wires to my hair and head to check my brain activity. All of my life, I thought I had a brain injury that occurred during my birthing process.

Then one day suddenly, around fifty-five years of age, I was not feeling quite right. My left top eye lid started to droop and close to where sometimes I could not see out of my left eye. The droopy eye lid suddenly seemed to happen and I thought I might have had a stroke.

Eugenia and I mentioned this situation with my Neurosurgeon and he ordered a C.T. scan. In a few days, we learned my C.T. Scan was negative. "Praise the Lord," I silently prayed. Then I asked my doctor, "why didn't my cerebral palsy brain injury, show up on my CT Scan?" He did not know but added perhaps my cerebral palsy injury happened elsewhere. Which takes me back to my early life, perhaps the doctor's did not know what condition my body had.

Yet, I was labeled at a young age that I had cerebral palsy because of very similar physical conditions. Without a medical condition there would be no real solid course of procedures.

With C.P. or not, after about fifty-five years of believing that I had C.P. but not as badly afflicted as many C.P. people.

The pain consumes my body every day of my life. But some days not quite so bad. My "rebel muscles" feel like being in bondage with every movement that I make. If there is a memory of this life upon reaching Heaven, I may ask Jesus. But in Heaven, maybe no questions will be needed.

One thing, I will forever believe is, the little boy inside me, will keep fighting and one day, he will be set free by Jesus, when I get to Heaven I will walk, run and then dance. Everything will be perfect. Praise the Lord.

Physical Strength

In my senior year in high school I was the shortest person in the class at about five feet. Mother and I were about the same height as adults. Dad stood five feet, eleven inches.

Dad's legs, arms, shoulders and torso was extremely strong and athletically gifted. He had the strength to lift or straight arm two grown men and pin them against a wall, one in each arm, at the same time.

And I wanted to be strong like dad, so I kept thinking of fun ways to create strength contests or games with myself, because I did not have the ability of playing in running games.

Our neck sizes were similar, around sixteen and a half inches. Both of us had broad shoulders and a deep chest. My strength in my shoulders and arms developed while hobbling and jostling around on my crutches for approximately thirty-six years.

The years of help from my mother and two sisters in doing my exercising played a major factor developing my upper body strength. One playful activity, I remember laying on my back, on the floor as if I was doing the bench press with my sisters holding my arms on the floor as I pushed up trying to lift them.

Other strengthening games was grabbing a stationary object, a gate, a sack of feed for the pigs and I would try to lift, move or shake. The feed sacks were much too heavy for me to move. And that was good for my safety. Yet, I tried everything for me to get my arms, shoulders and skinny bony legs a little stronger and these activities were working.

Daily, I playing my games with myself by straining, grunting, trying many different leverage techniques to move an immovable object.

It was an absolute necessity for the object to be immovable for my health and safety reasons. Certainly, I did not want an object to fall over on top of me, knocking me down and causing an injury.

Even if I was not injured, there was no way possible for me to get back up without several minutes or even hours of straining, trying to position my body with leverage or by objects to work myself back up into a standing position.

In my view, my brain never developed the skills to communicate with my physical body and to tell my body how to walk or balance myself while standing up with no help.

This was confusing and frustrating and sometimes I became angry and mad at myself and God for not making me like everyone else, who could walk. And I asked Him, "Why didn't He hear me and heal me?"

My First Steps

While living in the old farm house around the age of three or four, my Aunt and Uncle assisted in my very first attempt to walk.

For whatever reason, they were staying in our house taking care of my sister and me, while my parents were away for a few days. Upon my parents return home, my uncle, aunt and I had a big surprise for my parents all arranged by my aunt.

Mother came in the back door of our big farm house walking toward the big kitchen table. There she sat down in the kitchen chair, perhaps quite anxiously watching me, waiting.

Dad stood tall, just inside the back door, behind him on the wall was the hat and coat rack that held a couple baseball caps and jackets. Next to the back door was the kitchen cabinet that was built on the North side of the kitchen wall.

Dad towered above the bottom row of white painted, wooden cabinets. Quietly he stood, looking down in my direction at me, from the other end of the huge kitchen. His big strong arm and shoulder help support him as dad leaned on his left hand on the kitchen cabinets counter top.

There I stood, in the kitchen with the support of my Aunt's hands firmly around my waist. She steadied me to help me stand up as straight as possible on my tip toes, pigeon toed feet and my bent, crooked, and knot kneed, skinny, legs.

My Aunt was crouching low behind me with her knees on the floor, to better support my leaning and wobbly body and not fall over. Her warm breath tickled me on the back of my head and her brown hair tickled my neck.

"You can do this Lonnie," my Aunt softly spoke in my ear encouraging me to take my first step all by myself. This will be my very first attempt, to walk by myself, without holding onto something or someone.

Looking over at Uncle's smile and his blue eyes, he encouraged me to take this step. But I was still scared I might fall and fail. Yet, I felt determined to take my first, one, two or three steps by myself all the way over to my Uncle, a few inches further than an arm length away, in front of me kneeling and waiting.

For some reason, this was my defining moment in life, one might think. With these first successful steps, I could finally prove to others and myself that I was normal and okay.

My Uncle's flat top, butch waxed, blonde hair was perfectly placed on his head. Just like the men who wore this hair style, in the nineteen fifties. His tight, short sleeved shirt hugged his big, strong arms tightly, which were stretched out toward me, to grab me, within a flash, if he needed too, I trusted and felt as safe as I could be with my Uncle safely grabbing me upon completing my three step jaunt toward him.

"Come on Lonnie. I got you. You won't fall," I remember my Uncle saying as if it was yesterday. He waited and waited, seconds seemed to turn into minutes. But my Uncle continuously encourage me to take these couple very small steps into his big strong arms to safety.

Quickly, glancing over to mom and dad I saw their eyes looking at me with big smiles, hope and encouragement.

My Aunt was still behind me holding me up, trying to steady my balance. The white wooden kitchen cabinets were at my right side just inches from me. The only open area was on my left side. And I believed my Uncle when he said, "I got you."

For about the fifth time, nervously and scared, I looked into my Uncle's big blue eyes. His face and eyes were smiling and speaking to me, "come on, I got yeah."

Then I took off, as fast as I could go toward my Uncle. The first solo step, with my weaker left leg, went pretty good. My arms were swinging quickly and wildly, as if they were grabbing for something invisible to grasp onto.

My body weight was shifting with each herky, jerky, floppy movement with my silly gait. My tip toes slid heavily on the smooth linoleum kitchen floor but my leg did not go where I wanted it to go.

My forehead cracked hard and loudly into the hard wooden kitchen cabinet just as Uncle grabbed me before I hit the floor. My first solo step in my life, was a failure I thought, because I could not go three feet away from my goal in reaching my Uncle.

Then, I cried as he picked me up and sat me on the counter top. My head hurt but my crying was from the anger and disappointment, I could not keep my balance or make my legs work, to take one or two simple steps by myself. This failure crushed me, even as a young boy.

Mom and dad rushed over to comfort me and congratulate me on my first steps. But I did not make it, I could not understand why I was not like my sister or my other friends who could walk, run and play. "What's wrong with my brain and my legs," I wondered?

Setting On a Table Top

Setting on the edge of a counter, tall stool or table top was always very frightening, I did not have a balancing technique without some upper body support. Falling and hurting myself was very real, including setting Indian style.

My legs were too crooked and unable to rest on a flat surface. The tendons in my knees and adductor muscles were too tight or maybe too short. And both of my wrists were tight also. I was never able to turn my hands over with my palms facing upward.

My loss of balance made setting on the edge of anything impossible. When these muscles spasms occurred I was unable to keep myself from falling.

Falling down was not always painful. The difficult part was the long time it took me, between several minutes to over an hour to get back up into a standing position on my crutches.

How quickly I recovered, depended upon several things, my pain, the environment, the physical objects that were nearby to grab or crawl up onto, such as a piece of furniture, the crutches or steps. Chances are I would need help from someone to get back up on my feet because my hips and knees would be like a stiff board.

My neck played a major part in getting back up also. If I could crawl over to a piece of furniture and place my head on the object and I would use my head and neck to help balance by body until I was able grasp something with my hands or arms. Then I could usually pull myself up onto my knees.

And I would fall the same way, as a board would fall, stiff and unable to catch myself, support myself or bend my body to lessen my impact with another object. It did not take much of a force, a slight bump or body movement for me to fall down.

If you stand a board on its end with no support it will always fall. And we never know in what direction the board will fall until the fall begins. And once the board starts tipping, it cannot be stopped on its own. My body acts in this same manner with the many hundreds of falls that I endured over my lifetime.

My neck was much larger and stronger than an average child's neck, because I used my head, neck and shoulders for just about everything, in unusual ways, such as supporting my body, balance and walking. Every part of my body was needed to keep my balance, the best I could.

Many of my falls were painless, but some of my falls put knots on my head from hitting objects or the floor. A few of my falls cut my head open and had to be rushed to the hospital for stitches.

One fall, in grade school, I knocked myself out going down the hallway. Sometime later that day I regained consciousness laying on the cabinet top in our classroom with a cold, wet paper towel on my forehead, with my teacher standing next to me.

The teacher told my parents "He was running down the hallway." Well, I might have gotten in a bit of trouble over that. First of all, I should not have been "running" at all. Secondly, I should not have been "running" in the hall way. And thirdly, I told my parents I was, "not running."

Although, this fall might not have been from "running" after all I cannot walk, so how can I run? So the fall quite likely happened from my herky, jerky type of jostling, as fast as I could go, trying to keep up with my classmates.

A Young Boy's Game

During grade school and junior high school, I enjoyed playing catch with my grandpa. We began playing catch with an old rubber ball about the size of a tennis ball, in the living room.

Grandpa always set on the old brown couch that was covered with an army green wool blanket "to take the chill off" he often said. The blanket laid half on the couch to protect the fabric from wearing out and then draped up over the couch back, to cover himself up if needed.

The blanket was always tucked in tightly where the seat and back cushions come together on the couch. And closely to his left elbow was a small soft pillow leaning next to the armrest on the couch. Grandpa took his afternoon naps there. And this is where grandpa would always set across the room from me when we "played catch."

In my great grandmother's stuffed rocking chair, is where I always sat when visiting grandpa. To play catch, I needed to crawl on my hands and knees on the old brown carpet next to his old black and white television. The carpet was never vacuumed, unless mom would vacuum the carpet annually or so.

Grandpa was continually picking up little bits of crumbs or thread with his fingers off of the brown speckled carpet. He never wore his old brown, leather, high top farming shoes, two steps beyond his brown stuffed easy chair on the carpet. He always took his heavy leather shoes off and set then next to his easy chair that matched the couch.

Excitedly, I crawled on my hands and knees, because I usually did not wear my braces on the weekends because of my leg blisters from the leather rubbing my skin.

Once there, about fifteen feet away from grandpa, I set up off my legs into a kneeling position facing grandpa.

Often while throwing the tennis ball balancing on my knees, I would lose my balance and fall forward and my hands and catch and brace myself before smashing my face on the carpet.

Most of the time I tossed the ball fairly well in the air to Grandpa. As many young boys, I had dreams of becoming a Major League baseball player. Even though my crooked legs did not work, I still wished and had those dreams.

With practice over time, I could throw overhand, three-quarters and even side arm. Three pitches, I learned to throw pretty good in my condition, a fastball, curve and changeup.

The rubber ball quite often hit the imaginary catcher's mitt, without him moving his elbows off of his knees. My target, was my grandpa's bare hands, cupped closely together to receive my pitch. His elbows were always placed on his knees to keep my target steady.

One afternoon he caught one hundred pitches from me, with both hands, while only removing his elbows from his knees a couple of times to catch the ball.

There was some talent somewhere deep in this herky-jerky twisted motion in this spastic, tight body of mine. There had to be. It was in my genes from both of my parents.

With all my difficulty, I was pretty good at hitting Grandpa's cupped targeted hands with my pitches. Most of the time all he needed to do was close his fingers after the wiffle ball or tennis ball smacked the palms of his hands.

Side arm, over hand, three quarters delivery I could still hit my target with little or no movement from the target. Fastball, curve ball, change up, sinker of some sort, I could still hit my target which was grandpa's hands.

Nonetheless, in my imagination, I still believed I had some good decent athletic skills to be a good high school or college baseball player. But my mind and body just never worked or cooperated with almost everything in my life.

Jesus still blessed me somehow with this hidden talent or ability to throw a ball in my own way. Grandpas are not the only one who can play like this with their time, love, joy, understanding and imagination but I thanked Jesus for my grandpa that I truly loved.

Just as I did, with the ears of field corn, when I was feeding the pigs I could not throw a ball very far on my knees and remain upright after my delivery.

Catching the ball was physically impossible with my hands, fingers and arms without a sense of balance Grandpa needed to roll the ball back to me.

We "played catch" from elementary school up until my high school graduation, either in his living room or outside in grandpa's back yard near the wood house. This was a tremendous joy to play ball like this.

At home, I played my imaginary baseball game by myself, by tossing a tennis ball against the living room wall. There was a three inch steel lever, in the middle of furnace flue control box, on the door molding in the living room.

The steel lever opened and closed the coal and wood burning furnace flue that was down in the basement of our one hundred or so year old farm house.

Our old farm house, was always cold and drafty during the north eastern Indiana winters. The black flue box was about two feet high on the door frame. Coming out the bottom of black box was two strands of shiny black steel chain that went down through two small holes that were bored into the living room floor. The chain connected to the furnace flue in the basement.

On the floor next to the wall was a black steel register about fourteen or so square inches. The heat from the furnace came up through the duct to the resister.

When someone turned the black shiny cold steel lever the chain moved and either opened or closed the flue to the big furnace that heated our house during the winters.

This rectangular area was my imaginary strike zone. The top of the strike zone was the steel black control box that turned the chain to open the furnace flew.

The top edge of the wallboard molding was the bottom area of the strike zone or knee caps of my imaginary batter. And the black steel register was my imaginary home plate on a baseball field.

Crawling on my hands and knees across the floor to the other side of the living room about ten or twelve feet from the furnace register was my normal spot to play catch with myself.

And just like playing with grandpa's throwing the tennis ball against the wall and grabbing the ball as it bounced back at me. There I was in my kneeling position starring at the wall waiting for my imaginary catcher to signal me a fastball or curve. Then do my little windup on my knees and toss the imaginary baseball (tennis ball) over home plate. This was my game of baseball.

The activity of balancing my upper body while being on my knees while playing catch helped develop strength and coordination in my body. The gripping and tossing the ball helped with me opening and closing my hands and finger dexterity. This was therapeutic and fun at the same time.

Childhood games like these are the only way I can compete in sports. But baseball and running was an impossible. dream. Children need dreams to grow and learn. We need to help children explore new ideas and try to find other ways to get something accomplished.

There is generally more than one or two ways to seek something. We must work hard and hold onto our dreams. But when we dream, set positive goals and work on our plans. And keep our lives are changing for the better.

My sisters' hated playing "ball", the bat was plastic and yellow. The ball was also plastic but white. Just as much as I loved playing the game, my sister's hated playing ball. Of course, I could only crawl on my hands and knees to play, so they needed to crawl on the floor too. So I want to say, "Thank you for playing ball with me from the bottom of my heart."

My Leg Braces and My Sister

A funny thing happened during my surgery recovery on both of my knees in the fourth grade. During this time, I felt trapped or unable to move, with the body cast from my arm pits to my toes, on the mattress in the family room.

My leg braces were worn from my waist down to the heels of my shoes. The orthopedic shoes supported my feet and ankles. The dark brown leather shoes were heavy and with a high ankle topped style. Almost like a boot, laced with shoestrings. Inserted in the heel of each shoe was a flat steel shaft.

The purpose of these two steel shafts, were to support my leg braces that fitted into my shoes. With the orthopedic purpose of supporting and keeping my feel and ankles straight and not walk pigeon toed.

A shiny, silver colored steel rod went up each side of both legs. The outside steel rod on the leg brace went from my shoe heel to the dark brown leather covered steel band around my waist.

This band was about two inches wide and buckled in front around my naval area. Plus, the waistband ran from my right side hipbone to my left side hipbone around my back just above my tailbone.

There was also a leather strap sewn on both shoes, on the inside of the ankle area that wrapped around the steel brace bar and bucked around the outside of each ankle for added orthopedic ankle support.

My shoes were the ugliest shoes ever made, in my view. But I needed these shoes, to fit my leg braces so I could "walk." Every few days, I polished the scuffed up, shoes to help keep my shoes looking nice. My walking was odd, clumsy and difficult but "walking funny" was much easier than crawling on my hands and knees.

The brace shoes always had big steel toe plates on each shoe. Picking up my feet up off the floor with each step I took was physically impossible because my legs were stiff from the tight, spastic leg muscles. So my shoes dragged across every surface.

Usually twice annually, we needed to resolve both shoes but the shoe heels looked brand new, because my heels we always two or so inches up off the floor.

My feet were permanently in a tip-toes position until I was in the fourth grade. You could hear my shoes dragging across the surface from a good distance away with each step I took because I could not pick my feet up off of the floor.

And there were two leather thigh cuffs that wrapped around each thigh that were riveted to both steel rods on each side of both legs and buckled in the front. These thigh cuffs were worn just a fraction of an inch above the leather knee pads.

The top edge of these thigh cuffs were worn within a fraction of an inch from the upper Adductor Longus muscles in my groin area.

Along with the thigh cuffs, waistband, knee pads there was a similar cuff around my calves. The calf cuffs also buckled in front of my leg shins. All seven of these leather bands were riveted on both brace leg bars on each leg. All of these bands on my legs were designed to help straighten my legs.

My leg braces also had three sets of hinges on each bar or rod that attached to my waist, knee and ankle areas. On each knee joint hinge and hip joint hinge there were four sliding steel locking devices to lock and keep my knees and hips locked and straight. This mechanism was designed to force my legs straight and stretch with pressure onto my tendons and muscles. Just like bending your fingers backwards until the pain sets in.

But the leg braces helped make it much easier for me to stand and jostle around with my crutches up until my high school years. But there were also several things that I was unhappy about wearing these braces.

The steel body framed, leather cuffed, braces were hot and heavy to wear all day. The weight of these braces often caused me to lose my balance and I would fall down almost daily or even several times daily.

During the warmer weather days, I would get blisters on my legs. Just like saddle sores. My hot, sweaty, skin under the leather bands and cuffs would rub my skin. This skin friction quickly became sore and created raw, open bloody blisters. From one to six raw bloody blisters at any given time. This was very painful and hurt with each step or movement I made while wearing my leg braces.

Thirdly, sometimes the steel ball barring hinges on both hips and the four hinges around my knees would pinch my skin.

Fourth, the thigh cuffs were very high up in my groin by designed to counter act the tightness of my adductor muscles. And over fourteen years and much too often, my scrotum would get pinched between my upper thigh cuffs.

It was not possible to pull my boxer shorts up or down when they were worn under the leather cuffs on my legs to use the toilet. The braces were always tight against my skin.

The tight elastic in brief underwear often got caught on my leather brace cuffs or steel hinges and locks.

The boxer shorts with a snap above the fly worked the best for me, in regards to pulling the shorts up and down. There was nothing that we could think of, to protect my legs from the blisters.

My sister one afternoon, sat there in the living room floor, she was about four or five years old. She just lugged my heavy steel and leather leg braces in both of her arms from my bedroom.

She was setting flat on the floor trying to put my leg braces on for the first time, to see if she could walk with my braces. And she knew how the braces were worn because many times she would help or watch mother and I put the leg braces on me.

And my sisters also worked as a team to help put the braces on my legs, on some weekends, when mom was busy.

My youngest sister wore her long pant legs under the braces. It took her a few attempts to hold open the five leather cuffs to set her legs in my braces and my brace shoes but soon she had herself strapped in and buckled up in my braces.

She tried standing up as normally as possible, but she realized while wearing my leg braces, she could not get up off the floor. She could not quickly and easily jump up as she normally would as a normal four or five year old.

With the aid of the living room chair she was finally able to stand and steady herself. But her walking was completely different than her normal walking gate. Her arms were spread wide as if she was trying to balance herself on a tight rope or on a narrow ledge.

Whenever she lost her balance she was quickly able to bend at the waist and catch and steady her body with her hands and fingertips touching the floor. This was something I could not do.

We were giggling and laughing at my sister over the unusual movements and energy that she had to use to jostle across the living room.

Suddenly, I realized that her physical actions were as awkward with my braces as my physical walking actions were. Now those amusements were not so joyful. But she was willing to try something new and explore my real life situation.

It does not really matter what we face daily in our lives each person handles things a bit different in their own ways. But we keep trying to get better.

Keeping Up With My Classmates

My first year in school was not a "typical" first grade experience for me. Going to school was important but there were major physical problems, not only with my cerebral palsy but physical school building accessibility.

Most first graders attend their local elementary school. But the century old, two story brick school building, with two long stair cases would have been physically impossible for me to attend. Plus, there were extra stair steps leading to the restrooms.

The two times, I was inside the elementary school I remember holding onto the hand rail on the left side of the stair case leading down into the school basement on the wrong side of the stairs.

Both of my hands were tightly gripping the hand rail, because I was afraid I might fall down those long, steep cement steps. It seems to me, there might have been twenty or more steps in each staircase.

Going up or down the stairs always seemed a bit easier for me when the hand rails were on my left side. And this would always put me on the opposite side of the normal flow of people going up and down stairs.

It was more comfortable or secure with the hand rail on my left side because my strong leg was my right leg. Stepping down or more precisely, slipping my right foot sideways off the edge of the step down onto the step below.

My left knee was more flexible, so my left knee did the bending when going up and down steps, especially when there were several steps all together. Going down the stairs, I stood sideways facing the wall because I gripped the hand rail with both hands.

Once my stiff, stronger right leg pushed my right food off a step, down to the step below, my left knee bent and then I slid my left foot to join my right foot on each step below.

While jostling through all of these procedures to keep my balance from falling with each step going down a flight of stairs, I still needed a way to safely carry my two crutches with me.

It was impossible to leave the two crutches at the top of the stair when I needed the crutches to get around on when I reached the bottom of the stairs.

Therefore, I stood facing the wall on these steps, gripping so tightly onto the staircase hand rail with both hands. Soon my body began aching from gripping the hand rail very tightly to keep my balance.

Then I hooked both crutch hand grips up over my left forearm and let the crutch tips drag noisily, banging behind down the steps on the stairs.

Finally, after several long scary minutes I reached the bottom of the stairs and I was standing on a smooth cement floor. This smooth floor would be very dangerous from slipping, whether the floor was wet or dry with my crutches.

Down the hall in the basement, was a few more stair steps leading to the restrooms. Now I was feeling desperate, running out of time to get to the restroom. Hurrying a little faster on my crutches with my body locomotion, just made the fight much more difficult to move safely and quickly because my muscles would get tenser.

These steps were very dangerous, difficult and time consuming for me to manage with my crutches and full length leg braces. There was no possible way that I would have had enough time to maneuver those stairs, with my crooked body that would not work going up and down stairs several times daily. Certainly, I would have wet my pants daily or worse.

Going up or down a flight of stairs, with more than two steps was physically dangerous of me, from losing my balance and falling over.

My journey going up a flight of stairs was much different than going down a flight of stairs but it was still slow, hard work and very dangerous.

As the years passed, I did not want to be a part of the special educational programs that were included in our educational systems. A great psychological issue I had deep inside was, how could I be "more normal" if I had been segregated away from the normal students.

Certainly there were the state requirements of every public school curriculum. In my thinking, I believe I would have done much better learning in school with much smaller class sizes.

It was not likely in our school system in the nineteen fifties and sixties, a different teaching and learning system would have been implemented. For me, schools were too big and subjects were taught to fast. And I physically quickly grew tired keeping up with everyone and everything.

School At My Teachers Home

Actually, I never went to the first grade, there were stairs at our local elementary school. But a new school was still under construction in the next school district.

My parents and educators believed the new school would be the school best suited for my handicap because everything was on one floor.

Now, I was feeling happy because I would also be going to school too. Just like my sister and friends were going to school. But my school was much different. The "school" I attended was not a public school building with many steps with big blackboards in each classroom. There were no special education programs when I went to elementary school.

My very first formal education began in at my home schooling teacher's living room. She was an elementary school teacher. Dad quickly and easily picked me up and carried me from the car to inside the front door, to the living room, so I could go to school.

There in my teacher's living room, I attended "school" every Friday evening for about three hours, while dad went bowling. It was so exciting to "go to school" as my teacher cheerfully greeted us in her silver hair.

Mother must have fought hard to find a teacher for me. She persisted with phone calls and meetings various medical personnel and with the local Board of Educational. She would not allow the educational system to turn their backs on me.

On this first visit, "for school" I had a small grade school student desk that she brought to her home from a school, for me to study on.

Finally, at age seven, I was able to go to school like Carol and my other friends but they went to a real school and I did not because of my Cerebral Palsy.

And for a period of time, I truly was going to school in my mind.

The following year I "attended school" at another teacher's house. She lived in a small mobile home within walking distance of a local elementary school.

My new teacher pushed me much harder than my first teacher so I was learning much more on my ninety minutes weekly visit. Not much time at all for my first year of semi-formal education.

Understandably, my first grade education was very different from a full five day a week public first grader. Dad never worked with me on school work, my mother did all of these things herself.

But I always got the stern look from him when the poor grades were posted on my grade card. Mother helped me quite a bit, especially right after the grade cards were issued. But I tried hard to do my best in school with both teachers.

My Older Friend In Elementary School

Almost nightly, I remember being upset and crying at the kitchen table because I could not understand what my mom or parents were trying to teach me.

Every new math procedure was like an impossible stone wall for me to climb over. Even learning to carry the addition digit seemed overwhelming and very difficult for me to understand. Actually most subjects I performed poorly in.

Several of my classmates could memorize things after repeating things to themselves a few short times. But I needed to repeat and rewrite things dozens of times for me to pass a test or an assignment such as spelling, memorization and arithmetic.

How could I enjoy school and yet do so poorly and feel so stupid! My sister's did extremely very well in school. Maybe the physical energy of studying and keep up in school was draining me.

Mom and dad bought a small electric musical organ for us kids to play when I was in junior high school. Everyone thought playing an organ would be good physical therapy for hands and fingers.

My hands and fingers never functioned well, even with coloring books. My fingers functioned like a slow moving robot hand but never really sure if my fingers would open up, extend and grasp things. The tendons and muscles in my wrists and forearm were just too tight for this normal function.

Whenever anyone handed me an object, I had to be the one who picked the object out of the other person's hands. Even today, I cannot turn my forearms, wrists or palms up to receive something with either hand and I cannot properly shake other people's hands, which upsets me too.

As a youngster, I crawled around the house on my hands and knees. Crawling was generally done with a closed fist. Mother often reminded me to open my hands while crawling. My hands and fingers were often accidentally stepped on I crawled around near people's feet.

The next year of my schooling, a new elementary school was built in the next neighboring school district. This school was very special, there was only one step from the driveway up onto the main floor of the school. This single story school, seemed almost built especially for me. Again, this was exciting to go to a real big school for the first time.

During my elementary years mother drove me two miles to our friend's houses to meet the school bus, which was seven miles away from home, in the next school district. Every morning and afternoon she made this trip for me to commute back and forth to school.

At school my high school friend, and the school bus drivers and maybe couple other big, stronger high school guys carried me on and off the school buses.

My friend's house was about three miles away. The big two-story white wooden farm house also had a big wooden open wrap around country front porch. Setting on the couch in the living room of this big farm house is where I waited for the school bus to stop and take us to school.

Chuck was always joking around with me while waiting for the school bus. Soon bus rolled to a stop in front of Chuck's house, creating a big dusty cloud from the country dirt road.

Chuck quickly and easily picked me up in his arms from his front porch and carried me across the big front yard. While Chuck carried me toward the bus, I held my crutches tightly in my hands so I would not drop the crutches on the ground. Everything was going well and I was happy and excited to be around Chuck.

One morning Chuck suddenly stopped walking and he spun me around in his arms and he grabbed my ankles with his hands. There I was being carried upside down by my ankles and swinging me back and forth sideways.

Within a few steps from the school bus door, Chuck would stop and turn me back upright in his arms without dropping me or setting my feel on the ground. Many, fun, good things might have been said going up the three bus steps, between the school children who were watching Chuck carry me across his front yard.

Our school bus driver, was laughing and saying something to us as Chuck easily, quickly and gently sat me down in my normal front seat spot, next to the window on the right side of the school bus.

Mother also commuted me over to the Faust's house to catch the school bus the following five years. We always sat in the car in the Faust's driveway waiting for the school bus.

If we had a few extra minutes, mom quizzed me on my mathematics and spelling words. Once the bus started down the steep hill mom would quickly jump out of the car, scurrying over to the passenger front door and lift me into her arms while, then struggled to carry me and the book bag up the three school bus steps.

My second bus driver carried me up on and off the school bus at school. Sam always grabbed me around the chest or shoulders as he stood behind me, laughing, pinching and playing with me.

Surprisingly, one morning the bus driver reached for my leg and he pinched my leg. Then he acted like nothing ever happened. His pinch was quite firm and hurt, my grimacing face expressed my pain. But I did not say anything, I would return his pinch sometime and I was careful to not pinch him when the school bus was moving.

Some twenty years later, whenever I seen Sam setting down, I would sneak in a good, firm pinch on Sam's ribs, for old memories and laughs.

Falling and Knocking Myself Out

Every time my crutches slipped or I lost my balance I did not have the ability to catch my balance again. Then I would fall, topping like a falling tree, hard, awkwardly, and stiff bodied. Often, my head hit the floor, piece of furniture or other objects.

Nearly every fall I would get a swelling knot, headache and a nauseating sickening stomach feeling. But worst of all, after some of these falls, my tongue would feel like it was vibrating in my mouth after banging my head. My ears would be ringing, feel dizzy and have double vision.

When these feelings happened I need to lie down and sleep for a while. Once I knocked my self-unconscious in grade school. Then woke up with a throbbing headache and a sick nauseating feeling in my stomach and laying on top of the class room cabinet counter top. With a cold, wet paper towel covering a big knot on my head.

My teacher was standing beside me and said my mother was coming to take me home. She told my mother, I fell down because I was running down the school hall, trying to catch up with my classmates. Later on that evening, both of my parents asked me if I had been running in school when I fell down. Honesty, I did not remember if I was running or not.

From my early life from age five to sixty years later, I think it is possible but never diagnosed, that I may have chronic traumatic encephalopathy (CTE, formally known as dementia pugilistica, is a neurodegenerative disease found in people who have had multiple head injuries.

Symptoms may include behavior problems, mood problems, and problems with thinking. This typically does not begin until years after the injuries. It often gets worse over time and can result in dementia. It is unclear if the risk of suicide is altered. And suicide thoughts might have been subconsciously in my brain since the late 1970's.

Symptoms may include behavior problems, mood problems, and problems with thinking. This typically does not begin until years after the injuries. It often gets worse over time and can result in dementia. It is unclear if the risk of suicide of C.T.E.

Most documented cases have occurred in athletes involved in contact sports such as boxing, American football, wrestling, ice hockey, rugby and soccer. Other risk factors include being in the military, prior domestic violence, and repeated banging of the head. The exact amount of trauma required for the condition to occur is unknown. And definitive diagnosis can only occur at autopsy. It is a form of tauropathy.

In my case, falling and banging my head on the ground, furniture, floors, concrete and various other things.

Even today, my mind wonders, Eugenia mentioned she thinks "you are not even here at moments." With my anger, frustrations, depressed moods and maybe with my previous thoughts makes me wonder about CTE.

As of 2018, there is no specific treatment. Rates of disease have been found to be about 30% among those with a history of multiple head injuries. Population rates, however are unclear. Research into brain damage as a result of repeated head injuries began in the 1920's, at which time the condition was known as dementia pugilisticator "punch drunk syndrome."

The Second Grade

The first couple of years at the public grade school, the classrooms were divided by a restroom. This was convenient rushing to the restroom. But very dangerous on crutches, with the wet floors. The crutches would slip and slide and I would fall and quite likely crack my head on a solid object causing a big bump or an open bleeding cut.

Or the stinky wet floors would get my clothes wet. This always made me feel ugly and bad when this happened and I felt very embarrassed and afraid when returning to the classroom where everyone could see my wet pants.

And I thought about running away and hiding at least until my pants dried. But the best thing to do was to return to my desk, as quietly as possible. Hopefully not everyone would notice me.

When I jostled around with my crutches, I generally looked down to place my crutches in a safe non-slippery area, or along the wall, to keep my crutches from slipping and me from falling.

The biggest problem I had with my body, I could not get to the rest room quickly enough. The quicker I tried moving, the more difficult it was to move. My whole body would tighten up like a board and get even more stiff and uncontrollable while trying to keep control of my bladder. Then I started hoping in desperation with my feet to move my body quicker, somewhat like a kangaroo.

If I relaxed my body muscles to step with my feet better but if I needed to pee, my bladder would also relax and then I would wet my pants. And obviously, my fingers would not function well enough to unbuckle and unzip my pants, also not a simple task for me when I was in a hurry.

Nobody, had this terrible problem, I thought, I had the weakest bladder than anyone in the world, I hated myself because of the weak bladder and peeing m pants.

Good kids and even bad kids did not wet their pants. Why am I so bad and stuck with this dumb body, when my mind knows different, better and right from bad. My body just does not listen or cooperate with my thoughts, needs and wants.

My mind says yes on things. My body laughs and makes fun at me and says, "I am not going to do what your mind wants to do, no matter what your mind says."

An Upper School Mate

Quote, "I remember riding the school bus with you Lonnie ~ and I recall thinking: "this is the strongest kid I've ever seen." Unquote, my friend sent that in a Facebook comment to me, nearly fifty years after we rode the school bus while attending elementary school. In the early years, never could I have imagined the meaning of his thought.

It certainly was not my physical strength that he was referring too, from my point of view but perhaps the psychological strength. He was one person of perhaps everyone observing me from a different perspective.

My friend played basketball, football, baseball and perhaps track and field during our high school years. He was doing all the things that I wished to do.

With my athletic friends, I had a special connection with them and I marveled their athletic skills. Their minds had the ability to command their bodies to move fast, quickly, eloquently in whatever activities they were doing.

Their bodies listened and cooperated with their minds, that seemed amazing, yet mind boggling to me, when my body did not cooperate, with my mind.

Through grade school, every afternoon, I watched Jim, whisk past me as he jumped off the school bus, jumping down off a four feet high cement block wall. And sprinting into his own secret race toward his house.

He loved music and played the drums in our high school marching band and pep band. The only drums that I could play, was on an old cardboard box with my mom's knitting needles.

He was doing things that I wanted to do, play music, be an athlete and most of all to control his own body movements. Just as everyone that I knew, controlled their body movements, but I could not.

The reality was, I cannot be a musician, singer or an athlete. But the simple statement, "I remember riding the school bus with you Lonnie ~ and I recall thinking: "this is the strongest kid I've ever seen." This is such a very important, powerful statement and I thank you my friend.

First Time in Leg Casts

The first time I had casts on my legs was just a few months prior of my first leg surgery in the fourth grade. The casts went from my toes up to my upper thighs, to keep both of my legs straight.

This was certainly the most painful experience of constant excruciating pain for several weeks that I ever had in my lifetime.

Either leg could not fully extend, causing me to stand and jostle around, up on my toes and to have bent crooked legs at my knees and ankles. Both heels have never in my life ever touched the floor while standing, I could only stand in a tiptoe stance.

With these crooked legs and my zero sense of balance and funny awkward gait motion, always caused me to lose my balance and fall down with a stiff body motion.

The purpose of these casts was to help stretch the two ligaments behind each knee. One afternoon, the doctor and nurses worked quickly forcing my legs straight while applying the cast gauze around each leg from my upper thighs to my toes.

The pain was shooting through the ligaments and tendons behind my knees, and all through my body. It was if someone was bending my knees or fingers too far until there was excruciating pain, with no release in pressure or pain, then forcing my legs a bit straighter.

The instant the doctor put both of his hands, on my knees and leaned over his arms with his total body weight to push down on my legs and knees to physically force my legs straight, every muscle in my legs twitched with ripping muscular pain.

Thinking clearly was impossible as this pain consumed my legs. Instantly, like being stabbed or shot. This pain was not good for me and I began to cry. Mother and I both asked and begged the doctor for medication for my pain. But he never prescribed medication for me.

While in excruciating pain I laid in the front seat of our car heading on our long four-hour drive home, crying in pain.

The newly stretched tendons behind my knees hurt so badly, I could hardly see or breathe. Mom propped up my feet on her leg to help give some comfort, as she drove home.

This was certainly the most pain I ever encountered in my whole life. Mom did not stop or rest during our extra difficult drive back home. We finally, drove to the Emergency Room at the local hospital.

Mother and I again was asking and perhaps even begging, through my sobbing for the doctor to give me some medicine for pain.

The doctor refused, his reasoning perhaps was not to override the other doctor's plans, at my expense with the excruciating pain. With no medications or hope of some relief from my pain that over took and totally consumed my body, my senses and mind. Enduring this pain, for the next two weeks was something that I was forced to do by the doctor.

Our good family friends, came to visit us, within a couple of days after our return home. This weekend, I was still in great pain with each passing day, night, hour and minute, from my casts stretching my tendons.

Everyone around the house were busy canning fruits and vegetables from our garden. The dads were busy peeling vegetables. Our mothers were busy cooking the vegetables that we would eat later that winter.

The children were busy carrying out the vegetable peelings from the basement to the pigs or searching for glass jars for the fruits and vegetables. Except me, all I could do was watch.

The big gray leather chair in the living room was where I sat most of the time during the day. From there, I could watch everyone buzzing around the rooms being busy with something.

There I sat, beating the white casts on my legs with my fists until my knuckles hurt. Wishing and praying that the pain behind my knees would just go away. Maybe, I thought a little pain in a different part of my body might ease the exclusionary pain in my legs. The pain was so intense and concentrating on other things was impossible to do.

At my young age, I tried to understand why Jesus did not hear or listen to my prayers to help take my pain away, only made me more frustrated and angry at myself.

After all, everyone always told me, "Jesus can do everything. Just ask. Pray. And believe." You can believe, I asked Jesus to take my pain away and I believed and prayed with all my heart.

My sister and our friend were only about four years old but they were busy jiggling my legs the best they could. The jiggling seemed to relieve my pain slightly. They did a wonderful job at their ages but their attention span was short. Every time they stopped jiggling my legs to talk, or rest, the pain in my tendons and knees would shoot back with tremendous pain.

But what those young girls did that afternoon is still vividly fresh in my mind. They needed reminded often by me, to gently keep wiggling my legs. Nearly a lifetime or over fifty years later again, I want to say thank you Melinda and Robin, for helping me in that moment of my life.

The excruciating pain, hurt much worse at night, I could not lay down in bed. For nearly two or three weeks I set on the edge of my bed and placed a big heavy thick pillow on the black student desk top. There I rested my head on my arms on the desk top and dozed off with painful exhaustion.

My heels rested on the floor, while my legs were both straight, in heavy white plaster casts. There I set all night long on the edge of my bed. Before the pain returned and woke me up again crying for my parents.

This happened several times nightly, it was impossible to lay flat in bed without tremendous pain. The pain was almost like bending your fingers back to far and then pushed a little further back for two weeks continuously.

Stretching those muscles, ligaments and tendons beyond reasonable discomfort was the most painful period of my life. For the two weeks, this will never be forgotten.

On our return trip to the hospital, to remove my leg casts, my mother explained to the doctor in harsh firm details on the episode that everyone lived and suffered through.

The doctor quietly and gently looked at me, than at my mother and said, and I am quoting from our friend's email to me nearly forty eight years later, after that happened.

Quote, "If I had given him enough medicine to stop his pain. He would have been a dope addict by the time you came back here." Unquote.

This experiment, war, battle and pain was endured somehow and reflecting back, Jesus was watching and the casts did absolutely nothing to improve my crooked leg situation.

Often things, did not seem quite right or fair. Everything seemed to be so difficult for me. Once the casts were removed none of us could see any improvement. My personal feelings, this was not living with this excruciating pain but somehow l endured, probably with the help of Jesus.

In my adulthood, a fall became more and more dangerous, with the inability to bend my legs and soften a fall.

Another friend, once described my legs like, "air shocks," I thought that was a fair, correct description on how my legs function. My legs moved stiffly, slowly and they were difficult to move into different positions. Bending my legs was a slow deliberate movement.

Describing My Leg Braces

My leg braces was a big help for me in jostling around much quicker and easier with my crooked, jerky gait. But my braces were hot, heavy, painful and uncomfortable.

With my skin continuously rubbing the leather, my skin often developed several bloody raw blisters, like saddle sores at one time. Mom experimented with things, such as using a powder puff between my skin and the leather brace cuffs. We tried using old knee socks like a tube sock to protect the skin on my legs from rubbing the red, raw bloody blisters, this helped a little bit.

Yet, this was still very painful and hurt with each step or movement I made a while wearing these braces. At times the skin would be pinched by the steel hinges or the thigh cuffs would pinch my testicles.

But I cried in pain with each slow passing moment, five minutes of time always seemed like hours of torture time. My crying, begging and pleading with mom to unlock my braces to stop this pain did not always help. They doctor's believed this pain was helping to straighten my legs.

Before my Adductor muscles surgery in my groin area in college, I remember the orthopedic brace people, mentioning back in my freshman year in high school that my new mini brace could possibly be the first mini brace made in the world. This mini brace was amazing to me and I was so excited learning about this new brace.

The mini brace signified a good feeling, I thought, if my legs and feet "looked normal" I might feel better about myself. The brace specialists concluded, "Yep, just like the mini skirt, nothing below the knees."

My mini brace had a tremendous amount of resistance to counter act my knot kneed condition at the brace hinges near my hip joints. With my muscle tightness and pressure of my thighs pulling together, the braces help to control my legs and keep my inside knee bones and joints from rubbing against each other with each step I took.

One of my fears as my knot knees rubbed together and my feet crossing with each step, that eventually my knee joints would wear out and need replacing.

For the first time in my life, as a junior in high school I could put on and take off my braces by myself. But the socks and shoes was still a big problem.

The leg braces and special made shoes, in my mind, had to be very expensive. With these added equipment expenses in the family budget and I felt that I was a reason why my parents struggled financially. Mom told me many times, "that your sisters gave up a lot for you."

Actually, I hated that feeling and myself. As a teenager, I was not strong enough psychologically, to stick up for myself and tell my parents and the world,

"Maybe my sisters did give up a lot for me. But this is not my fault and I gave up a lot more than anyone else has," in my family, the freedom of movement and the freedom to be me. Sometimes, I hated myself.

Help With My Shoes

On the weekends in my late grade school years I started trying to get dressed and put on my own socks and shoes. Every morning mom got me up and dressed for school because of the short dressing time.

Dressing myself was a major struggle but I tried for hours and I did the best I could, working with my stiff spastic, crooked legs. My hands and fingers were not much better I never could reach my feet or toes without discomfort and total frustrations. My body never cooperated with my mind, another self-hate issue.

There setting on the edge of my bed trying to dress myself, I learned through trial and error if something does not work with a particular task, I just kept trying and thinking of different ways to accomplish my particular task.

My aluminum crutches I learned worked very well on reaching many things but daily I struggled tremendously to put my socks and shoes on my own feet.

"Mom I need some help with my shoes please?" My frustration and anger was beginning to erupt like a volcano at myself, from trying to put my heavy brown leather brace shoe on my foot for well over an hour and nothing good was getting done.

"Keep on trying," mom would yell. Her voice would generally be coming from the kitchen area, "I'll be there in a few minutes. Keep trying." So I continued struggling to put on my shoes, sometimes switching feet with hopes of some better results or something positive to happen.

Every time I used my crutch to maneuver my shoe in front of my toes that rested on the floor. Still using my crutch, I tipped my shoe over sideways, toward my toes on the floor with the toe of my shoe facing the opposite foot.

With the help of my crutch I took the crutch tip and pulled my shoe up over my toes until my toes touched the bottom inside area of my shoe at the heel area.

But often while twisting my body around to reach down and pull the shoe over my heel of my foot, the top of my shoe would fold up and roll up under my heel.

So now my frustrations was boiling over and turning into self-anger because after nearly thirty minutes or so of effort, I still could not get my shoes on and this anger often turned into self-hate.

"Mom I still need some help with my dumb shoe," I yelled again feeling very angry and disappointed I could not get my own shoe on by myself.

Untying my shoes and pushing each shoe off of my foot was much easier and quicker because I learned how to do that with using one crutch without painfully stooping over.

One time, after again calling mom for help, will never be forgotten, mom asked my sister to help me put my shoes on. Just as she helped me put my shoes on many times before, when mom was busy.

My helper quickly came in and sat down on the floor in front of me and pulled my shoe off my foot. This gave herself a good fresh start on helping me put my shoes on my feet.

For a long time, I had been working, or wrestling with my body to get my shoes on as far as possible. This was done by me twisting, turning and using my crutches to help guide the shoes on my feet, since I could not reach my feet with my hands. My helper seemed to fix everything but it was not always as fast or easy as putting her own shoes on.

She asked, "Why can't you put your own shoes on?" As she wrestled with my crooked, stiff ankles and my feet with my shoes.

There was no real reason to answer her, so I did not say anything. Neither of us understood why my body did not work like hers. After all she was only about five years old.

Thinking anything I might say, would only lead into an argument. So I silently sat there thinking, "you do not understand." Yet, I was angry at myself because I could not do things myself.

Sometimes, I even hated my body and at times, I too wished I was dead. These thoughts perhaps, were just the beginning of the subconscious feelings I had deep within myself, on not liking oneself.

With a few short seconds with her help both of my shoes on my feet. The self-hate always appeared when I needed help with the simplest of things. And I had the same problem with my socks. Just two more of my not quite normal feelings, in relation to my self-worth was burnt into my brain.

School Bathrooms

At the new school being built in the next school district, is where everyone thought I should attend school. My sister's school, had many steps.

The new elementary school had one step from the driveway up onto the sidewalk and three steps leading to the playground. The sidewalk was even with the school's floor. And there were no wheelchair ramps anywhere.

My crutches would dangerously slip like being on ice, on the wet floors around the urinals, toilets and water fountains. When I fall quite often I would crack my head against a solid object or floor, causing a big bump on my head or stitches.

And my shirt sleeves and pants would be wet and stink from falling in the restrooms. Then I would feel ugly, bad and embarrassed when returning to the classroom where everyone could see me.

Many times, I just stayed in the rest room a bit longer to find the courage to return to the classroom waiting for my pants to dry, so nobody would see my wet pants. And think about running away and hiding. But all I could do is return to my desk as quietly as possible and hopefully not everyone would notice my wet pants.

When using my crutches, I always look for a safe area to place my crutches. And I learned to put my crutch tips up along the wall or anything that was safe to keep my crutches from slipping and me from falling but sometimes this did not help.

Getting to the rest room on time has been a lifelong major problem from preschool through college until this day. My legs would not go fast enough or my fingers would not function quickly enough with my buttons or zippers.

The quicker I tried moving the more difficult it was to move. My whole body would get tighter, stiffer and uncontrollable while I trying to control my bladder or bowels.

My fingers and hands would not cooperate with each other or with my mind and move easily and freely with the buckles, snaps and zippers on my pants in doing this simple task.

The muscles would always become much tighter and stiffer when I was trying desperately to get to the bathroom on time. My body just never cooperated with me, I really did not like this body and I did not like myself when I particularly, wet my pants.

Have You Ever Fallen Before

Many times I have been accidentally knocked down while growing up. Usually I was trying to go to fast, or my crutches would slip on something. Or my playmates would accidentally bump into me and I would go crashing to the floor often bumping my head.

Some people suggested wearing a helmet to protect my head but I did not want to wear any head gear or anything that would make me look "more disabled."

"Cripple," I hated hearing that word. It sounded very bad to me, That word, which I did not like to hear or say, just reinforced my thoughts, that I was not normal.

As a youngster, mom took me in for a checkup and the doctor asked me, "Have you ever fallen before?" Feeling annoyed by his question, how stupid can he be? Countless times, I have fallen down. Some falls I will never forget.

One day at school, a high school classmate was standing by her locker which was next to my school locker and someone joyfully pushed my friend back onto me causing me to fall down.

This was no big deal, things happen and I was unharmed and several fellow classmates who stood around us quickly helped me up and back up onto my crutches.

My friend, was uncomfortable about knocking me over, probably embarrassed and she sincerely apologized to me. But it was not her fault she knocked me over, because someone pushed her into me. But from that moment on, we jokingly spoke about her knocking me down.

One very bad fall I had was at the local feed mill. As a youngster, I was standing on the pickup truck seat, looking out the back window. My sister and I were watching the workers carry the heavy ground cow feed into the back of the pickup.

But Then I stuck my head out the cab window and leaning out to get a better view on the men loading our pickup. Somehow, the door opened and I fell out of the pickup head first onto the cement on the ground. My head was cut and badly bleeding.

Mom was running as fast as she could, carrying me in her arms down the driveway to the mill's office. My blood was gushing out of my head onto our clothes and bodies.

But my most dangerous, life changing fall and injury came many, years later in

June 1994, when I fell again and broke my neck.

However, the embarrassment, these incidents are just a small example that was subconsciously building up inside of me over the years on my self-worth. It did not matter how much I wanted to be like everyone else, with my Cerebral Palsy I was still different, not quite normal and I did not like that.

Years later, I felt that many of these little incidents through my life would play the determining factors in my self-worthless and even suicidal thoughts.

Seeing Jesus

Jesus Christ is the one I have my faith in. Preaching about Jesus or quoting the Bible verses, I cannot do that, but I have read the Bible many times and I truly believe in Jesus Christ.

One sunny, hot, summer afternoon on our farm is where everything I had learned, heard, read and believed about Jesus became so real to me.

At this particular moment, around the age of seven, I was crawling down our sidewalk at our farm house. Like an eight month old child I was crawling on my hands and knees because I was not wearing my leg braces or using my crutches.

The top of my head butted and pushed open the old wooden framed screen door. And I continued to crawl down onto the hot, smooth, hard, cement steps and sidewalk on my hands and knees that led to my sand box, just past the milk house.

At the end of the short sidewalk was another steps leading to the green soft grass beside the house. Three huge maple trees covered the whole side yard next to the house with cool summer shade, including my sandbox made with a homemade wooden frame.

Mom and our hired farm hand made the sand box with old wooden planks that were about six feet long. The fourth side of the sand box was one cement block wall of the milk house.

For quite some time, I have been asking for a sand box to play in, And I was so excited to have a sandbox. Since I could not get up and run and play like other kids a sandbox was a perfect plaything for me.

This one particular bright, sunny summer day while crawling toward the sandbox, something very unusual happened to me.

There was someone I seen out of the corner of my left eye. A human figure suddenly appeared out of nowhere and he stood in my side yard. From the pictures that I see of Jesus, there Jesus stood without moving or making a sound, standing near the center of our yard.

This moment in time, change my life forever, first out of fear, secondly with awe at that moment and then with the feeling of wonder.

There was Jesus appearing out of nowhere standing in the front yard looking at me. Nobody was around in the yard, as I crawled looking in that general direction, a half second earlier. This really scared me for a second, this happened instantly. Jesus stood in my side yard, looking directly at me. There I was, on my hands and knees like a baby crawling.

Both of His arms were fully extended openly, outward toward me as if He was saying, "come to me." Jesus nor I made a sound. And Jesus palms were turned up.

There in His palms, I seen two dark brown circles about the size of a quarter. The scares when He was nailed to the cross. These two dark circles very noticeable like a healed wound and much darker than his long tanned fingers.

There I was, seemingly in a trance, not moving, I looked up at His face again. Jesus had a comforting smile. His long brown hair flowed loosely down, over and around His shoulders, fluttering slightly in the breeze, as did the long, white sleeves of His robe, within twenty-five feet of me. Jesus robe flowed down off His shoulders and stopped just above His dark, dusty, sandals.

After those few short seconds a car drove by then Jesus was gone quicker than a blink of an eye.

"Mom, Mom," I quickly yelled toward the farm house. "What? What?" mom asked me anxiously as she stuck her head out from the screen door.

"I just seen Jesus," I excitedly told her, "I just seen Jesus standing in our front yard."

Mom always said, "I do not know what Lonnie seen that day. But I do believe he seen something," I heard her tell other people several times. There was no "something" about it. My eyes, heart, mind and being seen what I seen, I seen Jesus.

Every time, I remember that moment I get chills and goose bumps run up and down my body. The hair on my head and arms stands up also while rethinking about that incredible event.

My Pastor often called this sensation, "God Bumps." There will never be anyone or anything on this earth that could change my belief on what happened that day, when I was a young boy.

That moment in my life, will be with me forever, in my mind, heart, soul and my spirit. Even through my eternal life in Heaven.

People may always ask and wonder, "Why did Jesus come back to earth in Lonnie's front yard and only showed Himself to Lonnie?" Or, "Why did Jesus not heal Lonnie at that moment?"

"What was so special about Lonnie?" An infinite number of questions can be asked and raised by anyone that wishes to do so. My only honest answer to those questions is, "I do not know why Jesus did what He did, when He revealed himself to me at that moment in my life. Or why Jesus revealed himself in that matter under those circumstances."

In my front yard, Jesus reasoning or plans was just about me. Jesus may have revealed himself because He wanted me to believe in Him and to trust him through my life.

In revealing Himself to me and with his unspoken gesture of extending his arms and hands toward me my belief and faith in Jesus Christ was so real. Seeing Jesus standing in my yard looking at me He spoke to my heart and said, "I am here. Believe in me now. Come to me."

Jesus Christ gave me this Spirit that I received at the moment I seen Jesus Christ with my heart, belief and eyes.

Because of all the non-believers who try to discredit everything in regards to my powerful moment with Jesus in my life I have kept this very quiet from everyone.

However, as an adult I only know what I know. The people that believe, do believe me.

In my belief and understanding the choice a person has, is ether Heaven or Hell. And I certainly want my family, friends and others who somehow come across my path to make it to Heaven.

This is one reason; I care for the people who I have touched, can make their way, through Jesus to Heaven also.

The purpose is not so important to believe in me but to believe in Jesus. But I hope people believe in my event, to begin their belief and faith, in the Lord Jesus Christ.

All we need to do is believe in Jesus Christ and in His Holy Spirit and give your life to Him.

Simple in many ways but life can still be difficult even as a believer. With Jesus in my heart, I have the Faith, Hope and Eternal Life in Heaven.

Embarrassing Events at the Hospital

Mother and I were waiting to see the doctor one day at the clinic for several hours. And waiting for the doctor, was something that I have no patience for even at ten years old.

We were setting in a small room and the nurse mentioned to us the doctor will be here soon for about the third time. The room was divided in half with a long curtain that hung in the center of the room, up next to my examination table.

The nurse told me to get undressed down to my underwear, as mom helped lift me up onto the high table. And mother undressed me, as requested by the nurse.

Quickly, boredom overwhelmed me in this total white room. There was nothing in the room except the examination table, chair and one old magazine, that mom quietly, boringly thumbed through.

Now over three hours have dragged by and the doctor still has not arrived. From boredom, I crawled back and forth on my hands and knees on the examination table, in my underwear, like a caged tiger. Several times the nurse informed us the doctor was right around the corner

"That must be a long corner," I said to mom she agreed with a nod and a deep sigh. A few "paces" later on the examination table, now angry at my doctor I crawled down to the end of the table and started toying with and swinging the curtain back and forth. Looking down off the edge of the examination table on my hands and knees, I noticed a green metal trash can lined with a white plastic garbage bag on the floor.

From that vantage point on my knees on the examination table, I could see a little bit inside the other room past the white curtain but I could not see the whole area. Slowly I eased out over the end of the table.

Grabbing the sheet tightly to steady myself with my fists to peek into the other side, my hands slipped and I fell head first crashing into the metal waste basket. The green colored metal wastebasket banged loudly with my head and right arm inside the basket, onto the white tiled floor.

Quickly, mom jumped up off of her chair and pulled me out of the wastebasket and set me back up on the examination table. And she asked me, "What in the world were you trying to do?" This fall, going over head first into the waste basket scared both of us to death.

The nurse came running in our room, hearing the loud noise and commotion.

"Is he OK?" she asked mom.

"I think he is fine, maybe more startled than anything," mom answered the nurse while continuing to comfort me.

Then we learned the doctor assisted in an emergency surgery on a little boy out in the hall, from an automobile accident. After hearing the nurses reason on why we waited five hours to see the doctor I was not quite so upset.

My second embarrassing situation also occurred at a children's hospital. The doctor was observing how my legs functioned and discussing my first upcoming surgery on my knees with my mother.

The doctor requested for me to remove my clothes and slip on a hospital gown and he left the room. Mom quickly undressed me as always, and she tied the opened back hospital gown string behind my neck.

Soon the doctor reappeared with about eight nursing students following him. The doctor laid me down on the table, examining my legs by how much flexibility, range of motion my legs had. This is what a doctor does I thought nervously as he explained my physical issues on my legs to the student nurses.

But I was not expecting the student nurses to see me almost naked. All the nurses stood quietly against the wall. Some nurses smiled at me, while other nurses were writing in their notebooks.

The doctor easily rolled me over on my side and removed my underwear. He continued explaining to the nurses about my muscle condition in my legs and buttocks.

My eyes were closed from embarrassment when the doctor flipped my hospital gown away from my body, while continuing to examine me. My back, buttocks and legs were totally exposed for everyone to see.

Now the doctor wanted me to get up on my crutches and jostle around, in front of everyone to see how my legs and hips functioned or did not function, as I slowly moved back and forth across the small room.

The nurses wore their white or pink uniforms. Other people jammed into this small room wore civilian clothes and medical coats. Everyone closely observed my motion, my skinny, boney, crooked legs, listening to the doctor.

Occasionally, I glanced at the nurses and a few smiled at me but others were writing notes and watching me jostle around the room almost naked. And soon all the observers left the room as quickly as they arrived but this definitely made another lifelong embarrassing moment while growing up.

My First Surgery

My upcoming leg surgery was very frightening for me. Knowingly at age ten, a hospital is where people were sick and some died. Surgery always had some risks but I could only hope things would be better for me when this was all over.

The purpose of this surgery, were to stretch these tendons behind my knees with the hope, to straighten my legs and "walk better."

On the eve of this surgery, mother held me in her lap telling me, "Everything would be OK," but I was afraid I might not wake up and die.

The journey on the stretcher seemed long to the operating room just added to my fears of dying. The stretcher was pushed down the halls by two strong, male nurses. Nobody spoke, as if everyone should be quiet, when someone was sick or had died.

Suddenly, we entered into a very cold room and I was smoothly pushed up against the operating table. Vividly, I felt the coolness against my face. My body was covered by a white sheet from my neck down.

My eyes squinted while looking at the big round bright white light on the ceiling above me. The light was the biggest and brightest light I had ever seen before, above the nurse's heads.

For some reason, I was not scared but I felt peaceful. Everyone there was dressed in surgical clothing. Although, I felt naked under the sheet but I did not care.

Then a nurse approached me and her face was covered with a white surgical mask, I could only see her brown eyes. Her head and hair was tucked up under a white surgical bonnet. Yet a few short wisps of blond hair sprouting below her bonnet around her ears.

She held a plastic gas mask in her hand. Her brown eyes above the white face mask smiled and gleamed at me giving me reassurance that everything would be alright. Her surgical mask also moved with her cheeks as she smiled down at me.

"Do you know what this is?" she softly asked. Holding the plastic and rubber gray gas mask in her hand.

"Yes," I said as well as nodding my head up and down. "It is a gas mask and it looks like a mask the airplane pilots use on television," I added.

"That's right. This will put you to sleep," she said softly as she covered my nose and mouth with the anesthesia mask while placing her left hand on my right shoulder for comforting.

After my surgery even in a drugged induced state, I was disappointed and saddened my body was in a body cast, from my arm pits to my toes. This I did not expect, a body cast from my toes to my arm pits.

The doctor later informed mom, that a full body cast was needed to prevent a "swivel hips" condition. But still I hated this full body cast.

"Why me?" I questioned this helplessness, feeling terrible. Now I can not even go back to school.

While recovering at home, my day bed were two small square tables, with a single bed sized mattress. The tables were placed in the corner of the living room. This is where I would spend my days for the next three months..

From here, I could look out the big bay window at the weather conditions, the vehicles go through our country road intersection and watch TV. This was much more enjoyable than staying in bed twenty-four hours a day in my dark bedroom.

But this life sure did not seem fair. Time and days seemed to drag by forever being stuck in this spot. Needing to use a bed pan and urinal is a terrible humbling situation. In these casts my feet were permanently positioned about two feet apart the only covering I had was a bed sheet.

As always, mother did everything for me. She had to, for me to have any decent chance for an education and a quality life.

Weekly, during my surgery recovery, my fourth grade teacher would visit me for a short while.

"I brought your homework assignments," while joyfully greeting me, "I also brought along cards and messages from every classmate of yours," she continued smiling.

Anxiously, I watched my teacher walk toward me where I was laying on the table. It was nice for her to visit. She brightened my recovery time too, I missed going to school for those three months.

Removing the Casts

Time did creep slowly but mother and I was finally back at the clinic. Several people from the hospital came out to our car to assist in transferring me from the back seat. Since my surgery dad carried me everywhere. He was very careful not to jam by toes against objects including the table mattress.

The doctor ordered my casts removed, soon a man walked in carrying a small circular electric saw designed to remove casts. The tool whined loudly and the steel saw blade spun swiftly.

"That thing will cut my legs off," I yelled.

"No," he said smiling, "this saw is designed to stop cutting once the blade reaches the cotton under lining of the casts. But the blade might feel warm."

The saw whined. White cast plaster dust floated through the air, as the blade vibrated my leg while cutting a nice straight groove.

"That's not warm, it's hot," I shouted fearful of being burnt or cut by the saw. But quickly the top half of the body cast that was a part of my body was lifted away.

My legs looked terrible with the yellow, dead, dried, cracked skin. My face wrinkled with my cracked, dry, dead skin on my legs. Quickly, I covered my nose from the musky, stinky, nasty smell from the dry skin and the urine that dripped and soaked into the padding under the casts, over the past three months.

My legs reminded me of the little girl's legs I seen at the clinic's a few years earlier, bony and skinny.

"Look. Your legs are straight," mom excitedly said, while the doctor and his assistants closely examined my naked body from my chest to my toes.

"Your legs are perfectly straight for the first time in your life," mom added with tears of happiness in her eyes.

The doctor swiped the thin steel stitches, which looked like window screen wire with alcohol. My skin was stinging as the alcohol seeped into the stitch cavity.

The four, six inch long scars looked nasty, ugly and wide with their bright and pinkish color. Somehow the tendons were stretched and reattached on each side of both of my knees during surgery.

This was the first moment of my entire life that my legs were straight within a few degrees. Which allowed both of my calves, thighs and knees could touch the mattress, all at the same time.

This was an amazing moment, almost a miracle and I was very happy seeing that my knees and legs were not so crooked, bent and twisted anymore.

Mother stood beside the examination table smiling but her tears rolled down cheeks, at the same moment.

Within a few long weeks, a lot of determination, hard work with sweat and tears and numerous hours of leg strengthening exercises, I was able to stand with both feet flat on the floor on my own weight for the first time in my life.

In the weeks ahead it was so amazing and exciting standing up almost like the other kids. But I still needed my crutches and full length leg braces, because the other muscles of my legs were not functioning properly either.

The Ride

Nearly every night and sometimes a few times a night from my preschool years through elementary grades, I would wake up crying and screaming with terrible pain from Charlie horse cramps in my legs.

Mom or dad would hurriedly but sleepily come in my bedroom and massage and stretch the legs as much as possible and I would cry even more. Eventually, the cramps subsided and I drifted back to sleep.

Many nights I tried staying awake as long as I could from worry and fear, knowingly the pain would return. Almost like a demon, that only works at in the silent, dark night, then inflicting the pain on my skinny, bony legs like being stabbed with sharp knives.

This must have been a trying, difficult time for my parents. They did everything they knew in dealing with my pain, including following the doctor's advice. Yet they were still helplessly watching my pain come back almost nightly. My parents never complained or made negative comments toward me.

"Why did I have all this pain?" I asked mom. She answered, "I do not know Lonnie. God only knows. But we just have to keep working on this and other things."

Perhaps Jesus and mother was trying to teach me a lesson in life, we do not know all the answers but Jesus knows. With the things we do not like or understand we still need to do our best.

As the years went by, my physical pain never went away. But now the pain also changed from muscular to arthritic, neurological and psychological pain. There have been periods of time in my life when I did not have much pain but not for long periods.

Sleeping was never easy, even on rare good nights. Either my mind was busy thinking or my physical pain kept me awake. This may be a contributing factor why my grades were so poor.

We try to relax and be comfortable, for me this was usually on my right side. But quickly like a gunshot or a lightning bolt, the race, the ride is on. My muscles shake and quiver violently, several times a second, like I imagine running a race.

My vision is blurred and my teeth are chattering loudly. The facial cheeks are quivering while my feet are violently banging and smashing on the mattress or against the cold aluminum bed rail.

The psychological pain is raging inside as if I am in a cage with these aluminum bars as bed rails on my adjustable hospital bed. My mind and soul feels trapped in bondage in this body.

Then this ride of severe muscle spasm, this journey of shaking throughout my body ceases for only a brief moment so I fight with my body and wiggle to find a comfortable position.

But in a flash, this body takes off again, soon I feel tired and exhausted. And I hurt all over, imagining like I have been beaten up or stomped on by many bad people. Every night I fight this battle, war with my body or travel this journey.

My electric hospital rattles loudly with these spasms. It is a weird feeling, to feel my leg muscles slapping against my leg bones or against other muscles. My jaws would begin to hurting from clinching my teeth.

My dentist mentioned my cracked teeth might have developed from eating peanuts or hard candy. But I believe perhaps my teeth might have cracked from clinching my jaws tightly from muscle spasms, Charley horse cramps or pain.

Almost every night, my sleep only comes from complete exhaustion.

Garden Tractor

My junior high years provided me with additional great challenges. A new school, was built across the county road from our farm, a five minute walk away for normal people.

This was also the same summer my parents brought me a garden tractor all operated by hand to mow our yard, grandpa's, friends and our neighbor's yards.

The garden tractor, a ten horsepower motor was everything to me at that time. It was my legs, an easier, quicker way to move round, my transportation.

Grandpa also had trouble walking because of "hardening of the arteries" he exclaimed, from farming with horses and walking everywhere. It was a joy to help him in mowing his yard around the house and farm buildings.

Dad made two metal brackets that bolted on the side of the garden tractor's body frame to carry my two crutches. Then it was easier, quicker and safer to carry my crutches on these brackets and I did not need to set on the crutches when I rode the garden tractor.

The other modification dad did was bolt a wire bicycle basket onto the hood on the garden tractor. The basket was very helpful in carrying my schoolbooks or any other things I wanted to take with me.

On the first day of school, until snow season began in mid-November, and sometimes even in the rain, I drove the garden tractor to school, with my own parking spot next to the sidewalk.

Plus, I mowed a few yards for fun or to keep busy during the grass growing season. The garden tractor was my transportation, I could not drive a car, walk or ride a bicycle, and I used the garden tractor to feed the pigs, drive down the road county dirt road to visit grandpa and other neighbors.

From the seventh to the twelfth grade weather permitting I was on my garden tractor going to school. The talk in the neighborhood was, they never seen a garden tractor that had so many miles on it.

Get Your Fire Back

Get your fire back. It is not over until God says it is over. Start dreaming again. Start pursuing what God puts in your heart. People are born to succeed, some are born with a golden spoon or a successful life that has already been given to them. But not the people I know and certainly not me.

Each little task for me needs to be planned to dressing myself, placing my crutches in the correct position with each step I take, to relaxing and speaking better. Throughout my life many different things and people, gave me the desire, the drive to do my best in life. But every aspect in my life was a major obstacle, a tremendous struggle in itself it seemed.

Society places these rules and guidelines that people need to follow. The system is not designed for disabled people to succeed in my view. If we succeed we must do it ourselves by tackling obstacles and taking alternate routes.

Maybe this is why the medical profession supports the nursing home or rest home agenda, which is to take care of the elderly and disabled.

For me, although disabled I am extremely blessed. But it is also important to keep my mind busy and active in a positive manner and the computer and the Internet has improved my psychological attitude.

Also, I need to work much harder than a normal person would. My struggles I must turn into challenges. There is not a normal bodied mentally sound person in this world that would struggle for an hour to put their shoes on.

Try picking up a dropped computer mouse ball up off the floor while being strapped in a wheelchair. This can be done through innovative ways without the grabbers or crutches, it took me well over an hour to do but I got it done.

Sometimes we need to figure things out for ourselves to make us smarter, less dependent on others and hungrier for our successes.

With the frustrations, anger, self-worthlessness and depression I do not have all the answers. But I do know when we quit having our drive in life or our fire for living and Jesus Christ in our heart, depression will consume us and destroy our lives.

The vicious circle of low self-esteem at least on the subconscious level, was realized through years of personal counseling. Major progress has been made with my self-esteem but often it is the things in my daily life that I must continuously work on and keep praying and asking Jesus for peace within myself. Yet the struggle is difficult and ongoing with each movement until the moment I die.

Junior High Struggles

The very first year that classes started at my junior and senior high school was around 1966, I was in the seventh grade.

Everything changed for me in that school environment. The restrooms were further down the halls. There were smarter students. And the added physical struggle of going up and down flights of stairs was very difficult for me. Even though many teachers and male students often carried me up and down the stairs.

Academically beginning in grade school through to my high school graduation was very difficult for me. In almost every subject I did very poorly in.

Occasionally, I would get a rare B but most grades were C's and mostly D's.

Immaturity maybe, perhaps my brain, but certainly the physical energy played a major factor in my poor grade. Truly I did try to study hard and I always completed my homework on time. Doing the homework was much easier than memorization or taking an examination. My homework grades, was about the only positive factor determining my grades.

My brain never seemed to function well in memorization or recalling things. My homework, paper work was much easier for me because I could take my time and search in the text book for answers.

Frankly, every subject I took, I had difficulty with. Memorization or recalling things was very difficult for me. Reinforcing the "dumb and stupid" feelings within me. Many times, I would end up crying because I was trying and mother was trying but I still "could not get it" in my head how the principles and procedures worked.

Dad never seemed to have much time to spend with us kids. The only time he intervened with me concerning school was on report card days. Every report card day, I was in trouble with my parents when they see my grade card, oh I hated those days.

After supper dad would usually make a brief positive comment to my sisters about their grades. They were Honor Roll Students all through school.

But I could never seem to measure up to my sister's academic excellence and to my parents hope, especially with my dad, at least in my view. Dad never put great pressure on me other than encouragement. But he always looked at my grades much longer than he did my sisters.

The pressure came within myself and not subconsciously measuring up when I was not doing well. Truly I thought, I was dumb or stupid because my sisters did so well in school. These not measuring up thoughts down the road turned into "self-hate," depression and maybe thoughts of suicide.

Never did I dream of attending college until the last few weeks of my senior year. College was for smart students, like my sisters. Being smart, was not me.

One grading period all six classes were D's and F's. How could I explain this to my parents I feared?

Honestly, I remembered dad's comment, "Can't you do better than this son?" Again, I was in deep trouble, feeling hurt, I let my parents down again.

Within the next few days our junior high school principal, changed my class section and placed me into a group of students who studied at a slower pace.

This was good news and I was excited again that I would be given a second chance in school to do better in class. Being reassigned into a "slower group of students", that did not sound good, but I wanted a chance to do better in school.

My sister, was in the smart section and I was in the dumb section that was my thinking. But that was not the case at all, this new class section was a good group of students and we certainly were not dumb students.

The second grading period in my new section went much better and easier. And for the first time in school I enjoyed going to class and competing with my other classmates.

My grades improved in the next grading period, in my six classes from D's and F's, to A's, B's and C's. My science class grade improved from an F to a B in one grade period.

For the first time in a long time I felt good about myself in showing my parents my report card.

Neither of my parents graduated from high school and I feel they wanted and hoped that I would do better in school. My parents never discussed with me how far they expected me to advance in school.

If I graduated from high school, I think most everyone would consider, "he would be lucky," perhaps that was my feelings too, at the time. My sister ranked third I believe, in our class of one hundred and six students, I was ranked round the eighties.

Mother just kept working hard with me in every subject. She never gave up on me. Maybe she was at wits end with me too at times.

But nobody stepped up, came forward and volunteered to help with guidance and support in junior high, other than, our junior high school principal. Or ever mentioned to me, "Perhaps, I may be of some help somehow." And this caused me to feel more academically isolated, "like who really cares."

County Spelling Bee

One of my most joyful events in junior high was competing for the opportunity to be in the county spelling bee, at our county fair or "Corn School."

There was great pressure going into the class spelling competition, because I thought all the contestants were smarter than me. Through grade school I was an average speller, but learning "PHONICS" was helpful with my spelling.

Yet, I was scared to death to talk in front of a group of people because of my distorted, "funny cerebral palsied voice." Many times, I needed to repeat myself to others or someone spoke up on my behalf.

Speaking was not easy, my throat, lips, jaws, tongue and breathing, did not always cooperate with me to speak clearly. The harder I tried to speak better, the more difficult it became. When I became nervous or excited my muscles became tenser. And it would be much harder to breathe and relax my muscles to speak or move.

Some children laughed, giggled and made fun of me, and say, "you talk funny' or 'we cannot understand you." Or if someone asks me, "Why do you talk so funny?"

There was always a great worry and fear within me concerning my speech and speaking in front of someone or an audience. Many situations at school I decided not to say anything at all. This action was not good for me either.

But one special morning, I was standing on my crutches and wearing my leg braces in the classroom, along with fifteen or so other spelling contestants. All of us were standing with our backs near the back classroom wall.

Facing us in the front of the classroom was our seventh grade English teacher. She was a small lady with gray hair. And there was another teacher in the classroom who was the second spelling bee judge.

The teacher smiled at us and said, "There will be three winners today from this spelling group. These three students will represent your junior high school at the county fair next week. Good luck to all of you." And I was feeling blessed, excited, proud and "lucky" to be one of the final three students standing to represent our school.

And I want to thank Retha who helped me practice the spelling words. Retha was a senior attending the high school across the road from where my family and I lived. Retha's parents recently moved to another school district.

Retha wanted to graduate from high school that she attended for nearly four years. Dad was her school bus driver during these years too. One evening Retha asked dad if she could live with us a few months until she graduated from high school.

In a few days, I was standing inside the county court house with the other county spellers and the word announcer, along with twenty or so other spelling contestants.

The announcer looked directly at me, while he spoke to the group and said, "If anyone does not hear the spelling word or understand the spelling word, please ask for the word to be repeated or feel free to ask for a definition of the word."

With that announcement all of us spellers took their prearranged order standing shoulder to shoulder in the center of the stage, facing the gathered crowd. If a contestant misspelled the spelling word they had to quickly and quietly leave the outdoor cold, breezy stage on that October evening.

This spelling contest was the first positive thing that happened to me since my handwriting paper was on display three years earlier. But more importantly, I was one of the best students on that particular day, in anything that I had ever done in my first seven years of school.

This was so excited for me to be one of the three winners in the junior high spelling contest.

Each of us spelling contestants were on stage behind the court house facing the audience. The announcer and three judges were also on stage.

There were three microphones on stage, one for the spelling word announcer. The second microphone was near the front center stage for the spelling contestants.

The third standing microphone was near the metal folding chair which I sat quietly waiting for my turn, to spell a spelling word.

The other thirty or so spellers rotated in line and approached the microphone to spell.

When it was my turn to spell I just stood up on my crutches, with my heavy bulky leg braces. And I prayed not to lose my balance and fall down. Then spell my word into the microphone in front of me and set back down on the metal folding chair.

Once seated in my chair on stage, I looked out into the cool dark evening scanning the audience and I did not see anyone I knew.

Several spelling rounds went well for me but many contestants have been eliminated. Silently, I spelled every word correctly the announcer presented to the other spellers. As the spelling rounds continued, I was feeling more comfortable with my spelling.

Finally, just four students remained in the spelling contest. One was a very smart student from my class. Two other spellers and then me.

Then the announcer pronounced my word. "VAIN", as the cold wind whistled into my ears. Sucking in a deep breath into my lungs I looked down at the wooden stage floor, this time not so sure on what word he said. My fingers hurt from gripping my crutch handles tightly from nervousness.

The announcer stood at the microphone across the wooden stage as if he was a statue, looking at me and then he glanced down looking at my spelling word. He was waiting for me to start spelling a word or say something while several dozen of other spectators waited from the audience.

But I still was still unsure what he said, V-A-I-N, V-A-N-E or V-A-N?

Again, I asked the announcer to repeat the word. He repeated the same word loudly and clearly. There was an option for me to asked for a definition of the word or have the word used in a sentence.

But I could not speak, I was nervous, scared. Everyone was looking and waiting for me. Finally, I guessed on the word I thought that the announcer had said, and took a deep breath and closed my eyes and slowly spelled V-A-I-N.

The announcer spelled V-A-N. Oh, I was so disappointed and felt dumb on missing a three letter word. But a few things saved me from total disappointment in myself: One, I competed and did well and lasted until the last short rounds.

My classmate was the runner up speller, not long after I missed my simple word. The spelling word my friend misspelled I think was M-A-Y-O-N-N-A-I-S-E and I did not know how to spell that word either.

But there were other good feelings after the spelling contests. That I studied hard with the help of my mother and Retha who helped me practice my spelling words. Retha certainly deserves a great "thank you." This taught me, even for a short period that I had to be "smart" in some respects to even compete in the county spelling contest.

Grandpa

Grandpa told me numerous times while I was growing up, "Get a good education. Then you can get a set down job and use your mind. You can't use your body and do physical labor." Grandpa had an eighth grade education.

Grandpa was a very influential great mentor and role model with his honesty, wisdom, integrity and the way he treated other people. He had kind things to say about everyone. He helped his neighbor farmers whenever they needed help.

As a grandchild around the seventh grade on until my high school graduation, I was blessed to have been able to spend some time with him while growing up. We had some wonderful conversations, he was a great story teller.

Grandpa's story telling was generally about his life and growing up in the early nineteen hundreds. Stories such as farming, walking behind the team of horses or how he "walked three miles to school" with his sister.

We had numerous conversations for many years. Weather permitting, I would drive the garden tractor a quarter of a mile down the gravel country road to his house.

One hot summer day, I remember one vivid conversation. We were sitting in the shade by the wood shed. His story was about the day I was born.

Grandpa began talking to me slowly. "It was a bad snowy day," he said and your mother stepped out of the back door onto the cement step. "Your mother slipped and fell on the ice," grandpa continued on quietly talking and recalling the event. "And you were born the next day," grandpa said.

"Your brain was damaged by the doctor using forceps. On both sides of your head there were considerable dents above the temples.

"You only weighed three pounds and three ounces," grandpa added. My birthing most have been difficult, the lack of oxygen to my brain is what caused my cerebral palsy, in my opinion but I could be mistaking.

Over my lifetime, I have never blamed anyone for my birth defect not even Jesus. But I wondered nearly every day, that something else could have been done to prevent my Cerebral Palsy. And I have asked God, "Why?" In various ways, Jesus has answered with His blessings.

When grandpa quit driving in the mid nineteen seventies, I was very happy to take him to "town" about four miles away, to get his haircut.

And he took his grocery list to the ma and pa grocery store cross the street from the barber shop.

The last thing grandpa ever said to me was when I visited him at the county hospital in April, on my weekend home from college when we shook hands and he said, "I love you and I wish you the world of good luck." He spoke as if he knew he was going to die, from probably a weak heart at the age of seventy-six.

As I left his lonely room, I leaned against the hallway wall and cried. Grandpa passed away three days later and I was so sad for many months.

Playing Ball

At home, in the big farmhouse I played ball by myself by bouncing a tennis ball against the living room wall. There was a steel black box with a thin steel lever in the middle of furnace flue control box mounted, on the door molding in the living room.

This steel three inch square black box had a lever to open and close the coal and wood burning furnace flue. The big furnace was down in the basement of our one hundred or so year old farm house.

Our old house was always cold and drafty in the frigid, cold, snowy north eastern Indiana winters. The black box was mounted on the door frame molding about two feet high above the floor.

The bottom of black box had a shiny black pencil size steel chain that went down through the living room floor and connected to the furnace in the basement to open or close the furnace flue.

On the floor next to the wall was a black steel register about fourteen or so square inches. The heat from the furnace in the basement came up the duct through the resister.

When someone turned the black shiny cold steel lever the chain moved and either opened or closed the flue to the big coal and wood furnace that heated our big cold drafty farm house.

Only a few times over twenty years I ever been in our basement. The steps were difficult and dangerous for me so I never had to keep the wood and coal furnace going to keep our house warm in the winters but my sisters often did. They started building fires during their late grade school years.

This task should have been my job and I felt so sorry and bad. And I could not help them with this disabled body of mine.

Often during the cool fall and cold winters my sister rushed down the stairs from their unheated bedrooms. And they jostled for their space to stand on the steel registers for warmth while dressing for school. My bedroom was on the warmer first floor of the farmhouse.

This little rectangle area from the wall molding, steel black floor register and the furnace flew lever of our farmhouse was my imaginary strike zone. The black steel furnace register was my imaginary home plate on a baseball field.

Crawling on my hands and knees across the floor to the other side of the living room about twelve feet from the furnace register was my normal spot to play catch with myself.

There I positioned myself up on my knees, staring at the wall waiting toward my imaginary catcher's signal for a fastball or curve ball. My little windup on my knees proceeded my imaginary baseball (tennis ball) pitch over home plate. Then I tried to grab the ball as it bounced back toward me. This was my game of baseball.

Tossing the ball to grandpa or the wall was therapeutic and fun for me. The balancing of my upper body while being on my knees helped develop my strength and coordination in my body. The gripping and tossing the ball helped with me opening and closing my hands and finger dexterity.

Generally, there are more than two ways to seek something. But first we must work hard and dream. And hold onto our dreams for life.

Feeding the Pigs

During my late grade school years, one of my chores in the summer months was feeding the pigs. A black metal toy wagon is what I used to haul the corn from the corn crib to the pig pen and I enjoyed this chore.

Feeding the pigs was a five minute, easy task for an able bodied person. For me, it took me hours sometimes to complete. It was difficult with cerebral palsy and crutches to pull and tug the toy wagon in front of the corn crib door from the tool shed across the driveway, with the use of a rope.

The rope was looped around my waist or my right wrist as I tightly gripped my crutches. With each step I needed to stop and pull the wagon along with my arm and keep my balance or I would fall down.

My destination was from the tool shed to the corn crib door was around thirty yards. After several minutes of pulling my wagon over the gravel driveway reaching my destination, I laid my crutches on the ground and proceeded to crawl on my hands and knees entering the corn crib to fill the wagon with two bushels of corn.

Inside the corn crib I set up on my knees on the knobby uncomfortable pile of eared corn. Setting several feet from the black wagon I tossed one ear of corn at a time, into the wagon.

Sometimes, the ear of corn landed in the wagon and bounced onto the ground, especially when the wagon filled up. Pulling the wagon and maintaining my balance on my crutches was a difficult task, as I pulled the wagon full of corn behind me.

In order to overcome this problem, I needed to step sideways and pull the wagon with my right hand a few inches at a time gripping my crutch hand grip and the wagon handle. Pulling a wagon full of corn up a grassy hill and over a big gravel driveway was almost physically impossible.

A rope I thought would be easier in pulling the wagon. Then I pulled the black wagon full of corn which with the rope looped around my right wrist while gripping my crutches to stand on. But I could only pull the heavy wagon full of corn a few inches at a time. The pig pen was well over one hundred or more feet away from the corn crib.

But I needed to develop a better plan to pull the wagon because the rope was straining my wrist. And I kept thinking to myself, mom would always tell me, "try and try again."

My brown high top brace shoes with steel toe plates kicked up pebbles ahead of me as they dragged on our gravel driveway. My shoes were dusty from dragging on the gravel with each step I took.

Looking back over my shoulder I seen two shallow, dusty, crooked trails on the gravel, dusty driveway that I had just taken with my shoes dragging on the ground with my stiff legged steps.

If anyone needed to look for me it would be easy to find me. Just follow the trail of my dragging feet on the dirt or gravel.

The old dusty eight-foot long rope was looped through the wagon tongue handle and I tied both ends of the rope together as tightly as I could with my spastic stiff fingers. Then I flung the rope over my head, down to my waist and leaned forward on my crutches and took small steps. The rope tightened around my waist as I pulled the heavy, full wagon of corn behind me.

After my hundred foot trek or so, the black wagon rolled past me down the hill crashing against the four foot high bare wooden old board fence and rattled against the steel fence posts.

My crutches clanged together as I leaned them up against the fence, securely in a safe spot out of my way. Once there the crutches would not topple over as I tossed the corn to the twenty or more pigs.

Standing beside the black wagon filled of yellow corm I gripped tightly onto the wooden fence to keep my balance. Some ears of corn still had the dried yellow husks.

My parents instructed me to toss the corn away from the fence. And keep my hands a good safe distance away from the sows because they could bite reaching for the corn.

Tossing the ears of corn to the pigs was fun as I imagined myself as an infielder or pitcher on a baseball team. My imaginary pitcher's windup, was imitated with my disabled body.

Leaning my stomach against the old bare, splintery, wooden, heavy fence, I could grab the fence tightly with my left hand. My right hand would be reaching back into the black toy wagon that was full of yellow field corn.

Feeling for the ear of corn with my fingers I grabbed a decent size ear of corn with my right fingertips.

Never taking my eye off of the target or an imaginary catcher's mitt, but in this situation, my mitt was a muddy old sow's ribs.

My target was the sow's rib cage while holding the light ear of corn in my right hand, next to my chest. Tugging gently at my baseball caps bill, I pulled the bill down to shield my eyes from the sun, just like a Major League pitcher would tug at his cap.

Slowly and deliberately I twisted my upper body and shoulders to the right, just like a baseball pitcher does going into his right hand windup. But my two feet were both firmly on the ground, my crooked legs, middle torso and stomach still leaned on the gate.

The windup slowly continued, as I brought the ear of corn back past my right ear. My left fingers were tightly gripping and squeezing the wooden rail on the gate to keep my balance. Both of my eyes were glued onto my target.

With all of my white knuckle strength in my fingers and my left hand grip, my left arm strongly pulled my upper torso forward, leaning out over the wooden rail, like a pitcher's stride in his windup throwing his ninety eight mile per hour fast ball for a strike. My right arm followed my upper body forward in the delivery of my ear of corn.

My herky jerky stiff throwing motion did not exactly whiz past my ear as I dreamed, like a ninety-eight miles an hour fastball of a major league baseball pitcher. The ear of corn fluttered and floated through the air, barely traveling twenty feet as if in slow motion.

With a soft thud I heard, the ear of corn hit the sows ribs and flop off her body and landed in the soft gooey mud in the pig lot.

Yelling "strike," right on target, raising my right hand in the air like an umpire before reaching back for another ear of corn, looking for my next target. The old sow grunted and found the muddy ear of corn and gobbled it swiftly down her throat.

A long imaginary out fielder's throw I also tried, just to see how far I could toss an ear of corn, which was rarely over twenty five feet. Unlike most boys, who could toss a baseball over two hundred feet.

My next target might be a particular mud puddle. Then I could watch the mud splash or hear the corn land with a thud in the mud. With every toss of eared corn I would try to hit my targets. Just like a baseball infielder would toss a baseball to start a double play. This was fun. This was my game.

When I fed the pigs, often mom would yell out from the back porch and ask, "Are you alright?" Realizing mom was probably watching me from time to time, from the back door from the farmhouse.

"I'm fine. Just feedin' the pigs," I would answer and thinking and playing a little baseball too.

Another responsibility, which began in grade school and all through high school, was helping wash the dishes. During rainy or cold weather I could not get outside on my crutches.

Both of my sisters were outside helping mom do the chores or the three of us washed dishes. My sister's done many other things around the house too. Feeding the pigs I would much rather do.

Mother always informed me, "Both of your sisters work so you need to work too." It was good for mother to push me because she slowly improved my life each and every day with all the simple things that other people took for granted. And I can only imagine some parents had their disabled child institutionalized or isolated doing nothing for their entire life.

High School Incidents

The beginning of my freshmen year in high school, I needed to use a manual wheelchair, recovering from my second surgery on both legs in August. This surgery was performed on my achilles tendons.

The purpose of the surgery was to straighten my feet and ankles so I would not be pigeon toed when I took a step or standing.

The second purpose was the hope, for the first time in my life I would gain the physical function to be able to raise my toes and the ball of my feet up off the floor and then push my foot down. This physical function was much like releasing the pressure on an automobile accelerator.

Prior to my first surgery, in the fourth grade, I never had the ability to stand flat footed on the floor, I stood and walked on my tiptoes. My tendons behind both knees were to short and not allowing my knees or legs to extend fully straight.

Being pushed everywhere in the wheelchair was no joy. But it was necessary because both of my legs were in casts from my toes up to both knees. And I could not maneuver a wheelchair with my arms.

So I was not liking myself and feeling much more different, than the other "normal students" who could walk and run.

A terribly embarrassing moments happened when a classmate pushed me into the restroom. Just recovering from major Achilles tendon surgery, I should not be standing up for anything.

A glass, pint jar was all I had to pee in. A plastic hand held urinal would have been very helpful. But for some reason I did not have a urinal. Maybe the hand held urinals were not invented yet or available on the market during the late 1960's.

The jar was on the wheelchair seat behind me. Nobody mention the jar at school, it was embarrassing enough and logically everyone knew my reason for needing a jar with me at all times.

There I sat in my wheelchair blindingly, reaching behind my left hip, for the jar to urinate in. But the jar slipped out of my crooked, stiff fingers and shattered loudly onto the tiled cement restroom floor. Suddenly, without a jar to pee in, angry and embarrassed I thought, "What am I going to do now?"

An upperclassmen seen the jar shatter across the restroom floor and he sarcastically asked me, "What was that for?" as he stepped over the shattered broken glass next to his feet with a silly grin on his face.

But I was too angry to answer his stupid question and embarrassed of the whole incident. Cautiously and slowly, I pulled myself up into a standing position by gripping the white urinal on the wall.

And I was still scared and worried my casts would slip or break or I would wet my pants at school. Fortunately, my casts did not break from my body weight and I did not fall down.

Immediately, I wanted to punch that guy in the nose. But I chose to ignore his question, out of embarrassment. Sometimes we need to be wise and keep our mouth shut.

Setting in a wheelchair, even for a daily outing was a big issue for me. There were situations in my life when I needed a wheelchair, especially during long walks. But I did not enjoy using a wheelchair, I thought I was more of a cripple and even less of a complete person.

Also as a freshman year in high school, I enrolled in the Future Farmers of America class. Truly, I did not know what I was thinking other than I lived my whole life on a farm.

There was no possibility that I could be a farmer with my cerebral palsy. The beginning of my senior year, I still had no idea what I wanted to do after high school.

My grades were terrible in every every subject. My thinking was, "What do I like to do or want to do in my life? And I could not join the military and fight in the Vietnam War.

Dad's Running Ability

Grandpa Shipe would share stories about dad's school years. Dad was blessed with gifted tremendous strength and athletic skills. He was on the high school basketball, softball and track teams. Grandpa said, "He could not run far but he could run like a deer."

Grandpa continued talking about dad while both of us set on wooden ice fishing tackle boxes in the summer shade next to the wood house on the farm.

Grandpa would say such things as, "Your dad only stood five feet eleven inches. But I see him, many times stand flat footed underneath a basketball hoop and jump up and dunk a basketball with both hands on the basketball."

As I set quietly beside grandpa in the shade by the old white wood shed, in awe at these stories, I anxiously listened to his stories and wisdom. Often he paused momentarily from talking, puffing on his home made, self-rolled cigarette.

"Your dad," Grandpa added, "had a spot marked on the fence down the road, one hundred yards from the mailbox. That spot was his starting line where he did his practice runs for the one hundred yard dash.

Many times, I stood at the mailbox, his finish line and timed him with my pocket watch, I figured every time your dad practiced racing it cost me twenty-five cents to replace the leather on his shoes."

"How fast could dad run?" I anxiously asked Grandpa.

"His best time was nine point nine seconds for the one hundred yard dash. And that was in the spring of 1951, with high ankle top leather soled shoes on a dirt track too" then Grandpa paused to flick off the ashes of his self-rolled cigarette.

"Wow," was all I could say thinking silently, filled with amazement. Wondering if I could run, I might be fast too, like dad, looking down at my skinny, bony legs, feeling a bit disappointed with my body. Certainly feeling inadequate to even begin to compare myself with dad's athletic skills. It was not fair for even me to compare myself with dad.

"He also ran in the hurdles, relays, and the broad jump events. He was good at softball and basketball too. But his main events were the sprints.

"And I know how and where he got his speed too", grandpa softly continued speaking, bringing me back out of my thoughts.

"How?" I asked in wonder looking at grandpa.

"He got his speed one day while walking behind me as a youngster while I racked hay into furrows with a team of horses. He has been following me all day," Grandpa pointed to a field behind the big red barn. "But this time the horses kicked up a bumblebees nest."

"About that time the, horses started getting jumpy and snorting from the bees and LaVon took off running. Completely jumping over the hay furrows, running like a wild deer and he was screaming, yelling, running toward his mother who was across the hay field."

"Grandpa continued his story slightly grinning reflecting on his memory. "I yelled at your dad, 'get under the hay furrows', thinking the bees would not bother him there. But your dad didn't take time to do that, I didn't realize the bumble bees went up his pant legs."

"Later, I figured he would be all swelled up from bee stings but his mother, who died while dad was still in high school. She took his pants off and mixed some clay from the field and water from the water jug and she made a paste and applied the clay paste on the bee stings. He ran around the field all day long with no pants on but he did not have a bad reaction from the bee stings.

From that day on, your dad could run, like a deer. I think that is how he got his speed," grandpa concluded.

"How far could dad broad jump?" I quickly asked grandpa.

"He could jump around eighteen or twenty feet. I don't really remember anymore," he answered. "That's about as wide as the living room", while I compared the living room in his farmhouse to a broad jump pit using my imagination.

One day, over three decades later, I asked dad if I could have his high school track and field ribbons, if he did not want them. Dad's track ribbons were neatly stuffed in a small, dusty, broken cardboard box, up in grandpa's attic for about, thirty-five years or so.

Today dad's thirty-seven ribbons are in two wooden frames on my den's wall under plexiglass. The dates on the ribbons are from nineteen forty-nine to nineteen fifty-one. With four yellow, fourth place, finish ribbons all in nineteen forty-nine. Nine red, second place ribbons and twenty-four blue, first place finishes.

If dad had finished high school and graduated, I can only imagine the college track and field, football and other sports scholarships dad would have received.

Another time, I tried to imagine and calculate how close in a race dad might have been to the great sprinters in the Olympics. In nineteen thirty six, the Olympic one hundred meter dash, was ten point three seconds.

There was no possible way I could really be fair to my dad, in comparing times with their running speed with each other because of the track conditions, training and running shoes were vastly different and in different periods of time.

Not once, in my life dad ever sad to me, "I wish you could walk or run." Nor did I ever say to dad, 'I wish I could run like you did dad."

With an overall picture of one's lives I am happy, that these conversations never happened. Of course, I wanted to be fast like dad but it would be extremely unfair to both of us to compare our physical abilities or disabilities with each other. Nor was there any other person in my life that compared dad and I with each other, at least verbally.

Dad could have been a great college athlete if he had not dropped out of his junior year in high school.

One thing might have influenced dad's decision to quit school. In my reflecting on things, dad qualified for the regional North Eastern Indiana state track meet to run with the best one-hundred yard sprinters in the region.

With another one of grandpa's stories he shared with me, he told dad before the race, "You better run your best race because those boys are the best in the state," Unquote.

After returning home from the regional track meet, grandpa learn that dad did win his race and qualified for the upcoming, one hundred yard dash at the Indiana high school state track finals.

"But there was one guy breathing right down my neck," dad added.

The track coach elected to not take dad to the state finals because it was a three hour drive and dad was the only athlete from his high school that qualified for the state finals.

In learning this, I think that might have been the straw that broke the camel's back, dad might have lost interest in graduating from high school. My thoughts are, "What type of a coach would not take his star athlete to compete in the state finals?"

If dad had graduate from high school, every college and university athletic department would have tried recruiting my dad from several hundred miles, in track and field, basketball and maybe football.

Grandpa also said dad could stand flat footed and jump up with two hands and stuff at basketball, standing five feet and eleven inches tall.

His events consisted of shot put, broad jump, one hundred yard dash, two hundred and twenty yard dash and the half mile relay.

In some day my grandsons ill understand what their great grandpa had accomplished through athletics.

There were times when I had some difficulty in dealing with my dad exceptional, gifted physical athletic ability, but he never put undo, unrealistic pressure upon me.

The difficulty came within my self-consciousness. How could I measure up and "like myself" when dad was a talented and gifted athlete and I could not even stand up by myself without assistance, or speak like I wanted to speak.

Through counseling, I needed to learn to "like myself" and separate my life from my dad with his skills and my disability. So I needed to concentrate on my skills.

Overtime, I think I have succeeded fairly well with my successes and accomplishments.

High School Grades

College was not in my plans as a freshman in high school. And I had no idea what I wanted to do with my life, until the fall semester of my senior year. My dream was to be an Administrator and work in the front office in Major League Baseball.

The smart students signed up for the college courses. During my junior high and high school years, most of my grades were C's and D's. If I had a higher grade, I considered myself blessed.

My study habits were not the best but I always did my homework and submitted it on time so I did try hard and retaining things was extremely difficult, I barely made it through high school, by the "skin of your teeth," mom always told me. Mother and others suggested I study business courses, bookkeeping and accounting would give me the best start in life for my future they thought.

Our newspaper delivery lady, even suggested I should study law or be a doctor. She said I was smart. Her comment and encouragement intrigued me. She must have seen, felt or believed in me, where most other people did not.

We only spoke occasionally at the paper box. That was a very short lived thought, with my poor grades and my distorted, funny, silly, speech and poor speaking skills.

With simple bookkeeping I struggled greatly. Falling further behind, quickly I was losing ground on passing bookkeeping with each class period. Working with numbers was fun but it certainly did not come easy.

My bookkeeping teacher tried everything possible, to get me through the class with a passing grade in each grading period. Including studying several extra hours weekly in her classroom, during my free time. Even then, I barely passed bookkeeping, maybe I passed on effort.

My sister excelled in bookkeeping, as she did in all of her classes. But she studied much harder and longer than I did, in her cold bedroom upstairs. She was on the National Honor Society in high school.

Something must be wrong with my brain when "I couldn't get things through my think head." Why was I so dumb?" I kept asking myself after trying so very hard. Honestly, I felt bad and stupid.

My attention and concentration ability was not as sharp or keen as hers it seemed. Quickly, I easily grew tired from lugging around my heavy leg braces too. And I looked forward to the moment when I got home from school so I could toss this extra heavy weight from my braces off of my body.

I Am Not Stupid

Around the age of five mother began taking me every few months to the hospital in Indianapolis and having numerous meetings with medical doctors and others. These visits always ruined my perfect attendance award in school.

On one of our visits the doctors glued wires to my head to take a brain wave test. For several weeks after the test, mother gently cut my hair to remove the glue.

On another visit, to the hospital when I was in the ninth grade, I vividly remember. This doctor came into examination room and sat down facing our friend, mom and me.

The doctor was wearing his long white starched jacket and he stated, "Lonnie does not have the mental ability with his speech and his other physical problems to graduate from high school. If he makes it through the ninth grade he will be extremely lucky." Unquote.

This news was very sad for me and I felt very sorry, that mom had to hear the doctor's diagnosis.

Mon and our friend certainly expressed their anger toward the doctor. Mom, "raked him over the coals and I will do my very best for Lonnie's education" as I often heard her retell the story to others when we got back home.

Quote, "Lon, remember our trip to hospital when the new doctor-in-training asked you what grade you were in? You said, I'll be a freshman. He said, "oh, this will be your last year." You stated firmly, "No, I'm going to graduate."

The doctor responds, "No, CPers never go beyond the 9th grade." You nearly shouted, "I'm going to college!"

I finally realized what was being said and came alive and said, "YOU don't break a balloon when somebody is aspiring! How could you destroy a person's dream?"

The doctor immediately changed the subject. "I was angry that he called you a "cper" and still hear him when I think of it. He had a lot to learn! Right?" Unquote from our family friend.

This news was very sad for me to hear and I felt so very sorry that mom heard this diagnosis too. With mom's anger toward the doctor, I often heard her say to other people, "I raked him over the coals and I will do my very best for Lonnie's education," after we returned home.

All I could think of at that age to say and to help keep mom from crying and being more upset was, "I'll show'em mom. I am not stupid." But every subject in each passing year was very difficult but I liked school.

My classmates seemed to remember things easier but I needed to repeat and rewrite things dozens of times in order to pass a test. My graded returned homework papers were stacked with my best grades on top of the pile. But within a page or two the passing grades became failing grades.

There was always a big hate within myself when student's called me, "stupid or retarded." For me, this just proved to me that I was not like everyone else. Not quite good enough in anything but in true reality I was at least "crippled." And thought I was "stupid" too, because learning some things never came easy for me.

Mom worked very hard with me many evenings, trying to help me get passing grades. If I did get a good grade in a subject through my first eight school grades, it was because of mother's help.

My parents purchased a small electric musical organ for us kids to play. They thought it would be good physical therapy and exercise for my hands and fingers, which never functioned well with my spasms and stiffness.

My fingers functioned like a slow moving, stiff robot hand. When someone handed me an object, I needed to pick up the object out of the other person's hands. Even to this day I cannot turn my forearms, wrists or palms up to receive objects.

Playing the musical organ, grasping little crayons, coloring books within the lines, was very difficult while I tried controlling the spasms in my shoulders, fingers and arms but it was fun and a great exercise too.

As a youngster before I turned five, I crawled like a baby, generally with closed fists. Mother often reminded me to open my hands up while crawling. Many people accidentally stepped on my fingers as I crawled around under their feet.

"And look at what you achieved! A Master's degree! Way to go, Lon!," my friend said.

Speech

In the speech and audio visual classes in high school, these students stood before a recording television camera giving their presentation as perfectly as they could.

The classmates tried to distract the speaker, by yelling, waving their hands and so on. These classes were always the loudest with laughter that you could hear down the hall while setting in another classroom.

Speech class would have been beneficial and great therapy in speaking with confidence. But as a speaker I could not handle that physical and emotionally.

Surely, I would have wet my pants in class from laughing with everyone or from the nervousness of being in front of my classmates.

With my insecurities I was less comfortable and felt intimidated with male teachers. Probably in relation to my dad. The speech teacher was a jolly, fun loving person. He would have been more than fair with me in his class I am sure.

Even with my funny voice my classmates would have encouraged and supported me. This speech class would have certainly been a great learning experience for me throughout my life. The teacher once mentioned to me he, "would have loved you being in my class."

Typing II Class

Typing II was another difficult class for me. Mentally, emotionally as well as physically typing.

In Typing II class our grades depended upon typing documents as quickly and accurately as possible. The error free documents received the higher grades.

My frustrations was, my fingers did not function well and often I could not control my dexterity and spasms in my fingers. The typing assignment needed to be completed on time, or I would not get the points for the assignment. The added pressure with typing and rushing, just made my typing worse.

The physical activity in typing was good and important in using my hands, fingers and learning the skill of typing. The grading system and competing with able bodied students set me behind from the very first key stroke. The teacher must have realized this but I just kept falling further behind in class.

These typing issues and struggles were tough but the important task is, hang in there and do your best. Even though we cannot keep up doing some things. Keep typing those documents. Keep on holding onto your goals.

When we continue on and keep doing good, in spite of our struggles, Jesus will bring other situations, people and events that will reward us beyond our imagination in our future. It is easy to say, "Hang in there" but I also fight, struggle and have great difficulty of, "hanging on" too.

We may be so far behind in the race that all the contestants finished running, showered and have gone home. We need to continue the race with our pains and struggles. This also means if one needs to stop, rest, relax, cry or redevelop their fighting spirit, then do so, but do not ever quit.

Right away, I had two strikes against me in typing class. My crooked, slow, stiff, spastic Cerebral Palsied, fingers could not keep up or compete fairly with the other non-disabled student typist in my class.

However, I tried not to make excuses. Every day, it was always the same story. My typing skills were not producing enough documents with relatively few typing mistakes to warrant a passing grade. My own body was always making me feel dumb and slow, I hated this body with Cerebral Palsy.

At the end of every grading period I was in the guidance counselor's office explaining to him about my poor grades. And I did not goof off, I was trying my very best in school. But it never seemed good enough. Believe me it was no fun explaining to dad my poor grades or feeling dumb.

Somehow I made it through high school, with hard work and with the help of my guidance counselor. And I never knew what he discussed with my teachers but he always managed to keep me from failing several classes in high school.

Physical Education

Our physical education teacher was another person in junior high school that I admired and respected deeply. He taught history, geography and physical education. And I knew him earlier teaching at my elementary school.

He was a big strong man in my opinion, with black hair, a big wide chest and big strong athletic legs about as big as tree trunks I thought. Also, just like my dad's chest and legs big, strong and muscular.

He took long strides with each step and his body sort of bounced up and down along with his gait. If I could have walked as a normal person, I might have imitated his long, bouncing strut. And he always had a jolly attitude and a big smile on his face.

Every Monday he announced with his big smile, "Friday we are going to have a party in class." All of us students cheered until we learned his version of a party was a quiz or exam.

Quizzes or tests I hated, I felt so dumb, yet I could almost recall the page number a particular question came from but not the answers. But doing my homework was much less stressful.

He was a stern teacher in my view but he had his funny, joyful moments also. Many times he would have the class roaring with laughter with his jokes, comments or mannerisms at the end of the school day when everything formally was finished.

One afternoon, just before the bell rang to dismiss class for the day, He was setting on top of the teacher's desk in his tight black slacks. His big muscular legs dangling and his feet swing to his jolly mood. All of us students were in an uproar with laughter in the closing moments of his class. Including me, and if I got to laughing to hard or too much, I would usually wet my pants.

Then one of my classmates from across the room said something funny. All of the students in the school room roared again with laughter. Then our teacher added another funny comment and the class laughed louder, including me.

With this laughter, I wet my pants setting at my student desk. Too often my bladder would just lose control with my laughter.

We only a few minutes before school was dismissed for the day, I quickly thought I would just set at my desk until all of my classmates left the room. Then I would be alone in the classroom and hall way. And I hoped that nobody would notice that I wet my pants.

Then at that moment, the schools PA clicked on from the Principal's office. A woman's voice came from the classroom PA speaker. "Yes, ma'am," he answered loudly with total silence from us students.

"Would you send Lonnie Shipe down to the Health Clinic please?" The woman asked over the speaker. "Yes, ma'am," he replied.

At that moment, I wished that I had just died. My classmates roared loudly once again, when they all turned and looked at my somber, fearful look on my face. My classmate were waiting for me to get up and leave the classroom.

Just a brief few seconds earlier, I had planned on being the last student to leave the classroom, but now I must be the first student to leave, in front of everyone.

My desk was about five rows of desks from the class room door. Here I sat petrified, really afraid that my friends and classmates would see me with wet pants then laugh and make fun of me.

Everyone seen my wet pants all on my backside and down both pant legs. Soaking wet pants but what could I do. Never, did I wet my pants on purpose; I hated myself over this lack of control. Those thoughts certainly did not help my humiliated feeling.

From humiliation I thought I was going to die, as I slowly got up and jostled on my crutches The class roared again with laughter before I left my seat from the humiliating expression on my face. Not one person to this day has anyone made a comment about that humiliating situation.

As I jostled down the hall with my crutches and leg braces, a classmate struggled with how he was going to carry me down two flights of stairs without getting himself wet from my wet pants.

Finally I wobbled into the clinic, filled with ugly thoughts and fear of humiliation to see why the school nurse wanted to see me during this terrible moment.

In the clinic, the school nurse and the county nurse who I had known from previous meetings were there. She come to school to check up on me.

Standing in front of the two nurses, with my eyes down cast. Humiliated and actually hating myself in soaking wet blue jeans. And expecting someone to say something about "my accident" but neither one of the nurses said anything.

Finally, after a quick moment, but time seemed like an eternity, one of the nurses finally spoke and smiled while asking if I would walk around the small clinic room. She continued on saying they wanted to observe me walking and see how I was doing.

Embarrassingly, I jostled around the small clinic with my crutches and braces, wet pants, always looking down at the tile floor. Slowly in small circles with my cerebral palsied mannerisms, I hobbled around on my stiff, tight legs the best I could.

My thinking was getting away and hiding from people feeling like I was going to die. The nurses observed everything as I waited for their approval to be dismissed.

Understandably, my body was different from everyone. Yet, I could not understand why I was also punished for having a weak bladder too.

While attending college, I struggled greatly trying to get my psychological, "self-worth" understood during my counseling sessions with Bernie.

My psychological issues of self-worth ran much deeper and more complex, beyond my bladder control. Several self-worthless issues, were mainly self-imposed issues that started developing, most likely as a little boy into my adulthood.

Never was I abused or neglected while growing up. But I still did not believe at times in situations where I could not speak clearly, get dressed by myself, unable to tie my own shoes, or unable to control my muscles and bladder that I was still a decent good person.

And I could never be the person, I wanted to be with his body. But the worthlessness feelings of me continued to fester and then the self-hate took control of me over time.

A Bad Moment Turned Good

The friendships that I had were a blessing. But there were a few other people that helped me along the way also in a different manner, with negative reinforcement.

My poor grades were a major struggle and problem for me. This was probably well known throughout junior high and high school with teachers and administrators. One particular moment, near my high school graduation, an unnecessary comment was made by one of my teachers as he walked near me in the hallway.

When this teacher asked me, Quote, "What are you going to do after graduation?"

"I am going to college", I answered. "You will never make it through college", he stated and he turned and walked away, down the hall.

This made me upset and angry to hear that and I will never forget his comments toward me. He was certainly respected because he was a teacher but he was not admired by me. But he had the facts to back up his comment, the poor grades on my report card.

His comment was burned in my mind for life, unlike his lectures that he gave us students. Desperately I wanted to use his comment, "you will never make it" comment to prove him wrong. At the same time, I believe his opinion was not intended to be mean toward me.

True, I had difficulty in school. And he was a college graduate. He knew what college entailed and I had no idea what college was all about, other than studying. My junior high and high school poor grades and my lack of maturity gave him proof for his opinion.

Yet he did not know how my heart and attitude would change that summer. He ignited a burning desire to prove to myself and all the other people who doubted my ability to be a decent, average college student. But I knew I was not smart or brainy. All I just wanted to do at that time of my life was go to college, to follow my dreams.

And I did not want to give all the negative medical doctors, the professional educators or anyone else the glory, the satisfaction, if they were right, I would not make it through college.

If I see this teacher again and if I had the opportunity I might tell him how he inspired me throughout my college career.

But no thanks, there would be no joy or satisfaction to see him walk away from me, or to explain himself the second time. Knowing that I proved to him and all the other professional people that I was not only capable of going to college but graduate with honors.

Now, if he makes a comment such as, "I said that to inspire you." Probably, I could call him a liar.

But I might say, "There was nothing inspirational about your comment." The meaning of your comment was all bad, however a hot burning fire exploded inside me, to just prove you wrong. Thank you for that because I might not have made it through college otherwise.

But now forty-five years after my May 1971 high school graduation, almost to the same week on May 23, 2016, is it not strange or perhaps God's intervention to remind me to perhaps not forget but to forgive his comments.

And I learned forty-five later through a third party this teacher had all good things to say and even mentioned how some of the older male students would pick you and to carry you or down the stairs while another would carry your crutches.

He said to say hello and give you his best. He asked about where you are and how you were doing. I filled him in to the best of my knowledge. See....even he has memories of friends taking care of you. Not because they were told to, because they "cared'.

Debra my friend continued her Facebook comment, "I did fill him in on where you lived, that you were married and had a grandson and of your unfortunate fall. Also told him you were in the process of writing a book. He is just turning 70. Can you believe that? Only actually 8-10 years older than us. Just wanted you to know of one more person that you touched the life of and hold memories of you." Unquote.

Lonnie E. Shipe "Double Like" on your comment Debra, Now I am thinking of updating my entry in my writing of him to a positive feeling, thanks to you.

Debra, "Yes. That's why I wanted to tell of him mentioning how guys would carry you up the stairs here the athletes would help you onto the field. You have many friends here!!!

Lonnie E. Shipe "Yes, yes I know, thank God," Unquote.

My original reason on reconnecting with my teacher is stated above. However, after thinking and reflecting on the kindness, helpfulness of Debra we must forgive and forget. The negative issue was turned into a positive issue.

This is what Jesus would want everyone to do, forget, forgive and move on. We may not forget but we can forgive and maybe find some peace and joy with time and maybe turn a negative moment into motivation and an inspiration.

My Admired Teacher

During the fall semester of my freshmen year of high school my classmates always pushed me in a wheelchair because I was recovering from my ankle surgeries from a month earlier.

This is my second time using a wheelchair for anything and I did not like being association with a wheelchair. Using a wheelchair on a daily basis was an added worthless, helpless, negative issue for me.

The wheelchair just set me further behind in life, in my thinking. And I just felt "more of a cripple." and not being a complete good person

For some reason, I always had more difficulty speaking to this teacher, maybe I was trying extra hard to impress him. But my speech would not cooperate.

Basically it was all about being unable to relax my face and body and breathe properly. My speech along with my body I hated He always concentrated extra hard on what I was saying. Including with his body language, tilting of his head and moving closer to understand my speech.

Perhaps he had great difficulty in understanding my "funny, silly, ugly speech." But I believe teachers and adults did concentrate more to understand me.

And I was afraid to talk in class because someone might laugh or not understand me. Class participation was important but difficult. Yet I needed the confidence to raise my hand and talk but this did not happen for several more years.

When my breathing became easier and my jaws and facial muscles relaxed I could speak a little better. But I still hated my funny cerebral palsied voice.

The health class I should have excelled in, to learn how our bodies function. But like most of my classes, my final grade was a D. Many times, I wondered, if I even deserved a passing grade, or were my teachers just passing me along after all.

Who knows what I had done if I did not graduate from high school. Many handicapped adults live in nursing homes and work at local community sheltered workshops. That could have easily been my life if I have not graduated.

But my high school diploma could not guarantee I would not end up living in that environment. Which would have destroyed the meaning of living I am sure.

Changing the classroom settings, smaller classes to help influence me and have more positive reinforcement, to help develop my confidence, I might have have been a better student. Perhaps, a slower structured plan of teaching and learning.

This was impossible for financial reasons, time and maybe the lack of special education programs was available like this. After all, I was the only physically disabled student on campus. And I did not want to be associated with special education either. So the final decision was, I needed to be the person to make my life better, not anyone else,

Mother and many other people invested a great amount of work into every aspect of my life and future for me not to be institutionalized. Mom always fought on my side to better my life. In each and every way possible.

In another situation this special teacher and coach gave me one of my happiest moments in high school, besides being on the baseball team and my high school graduation.

One day during my lunch period in my junior year I jostled my way slowly through the gym toward the basketball coach in my leg braces and crutches and I asked him.

"If I could be on the basketball team as a statistician." Immediately, he gave me permission. Many players and friends on the baseball team played basketball and earned their red, white and black varsity school athletic jacket.

Dad earned his athletic jacket from his high school in the early 1950's, in track and field, basketball and softball. As a teenager, I remember wearing dad's green and white varsity jacket which had a big green and white "M" on the left chest area.

"What do I need to do to letter in basketball" I asked the coach. He replied saying that, "You must attend practice, the games and be helpful. Just like everyone else on the team in order to be awarded a varsity athletic jacket."

Late in the spring of 1971, my senior year, my special coach, and later my longtime friend awarded me my high school athletic jacket in the school's gymnasium. We excitedly stood facing each other with a hand shake and a smile and a standing ovation from the students. .

My high school varsity athletic jacket is still here, hanging in my clothes closet, almost fifty years later. The arm pit area of my jacket is a bit worn out from wear from my crutch rubber arm pit pads. Maybe someday my grandchildren will have my old, worn athletic jacket.

Our friendships, respect and admiration for each other grew larger over the years. Our paths have crossed with my surgeries, home visits, my wedding and other things.

A Special Evening

During my high school years, I did not have a girlfriend or marriage thoughts. Although I wanted a special female friend to be around and to talk too. It was not helpful in not having a driver's license, a job, a car, nor the money and quite frankly, the maturity for dating. My interaction with women was non-existent outside the classrooms.

And I felt left out in dating. One evening Allen approached me and asked, "Why don't you ask one of our classmates to the junior – Senior Prom? Allen spoke kindly and softly about our classmate. Instantly, I knew who Allen was talking about,

My shyness overwhelmed me. Oh I was so nervous, I could hardly talk or get my legs to move and jostle over to her on my crutches. But I was determined to ask her our classmate to be my date to the prom and I might have stammered at bit but maybe not.

It was a wonderful moment in my life, when she accepted my prom date verbal invitation. Oh, I was so excited, I do not remember much until the next morning in school. My prom date was all smiles and I think all of my classmates, including myself were smiling and happy, that my date and I were going to the prom,

Mother provided the transportation for us. During the prom several classmates and teachers came to greet us, as we sat, talked and watched the evening events, I believe both of us had a great evening.

No Excuses College

Senior College Day arrived at high school in the spring of 1971. After listening to several representatives from big colleges, I realized a big college would not be good for me. A small private college would be more costly but a local junior college might be a good decision to start.

In the beginning, I had no idea how I was going to manage living on campus. But I wanted to go to college. Stairs, steps, close restrooms and the winter environment was my concerns. When I could not manage the two flights of stairs in high school without a great physical strain, difficulty, energy and time.

There was no physical way possible that I could venture out on a college campus on crutches and handle the steps, carry my books, with the ice, snow, rain and still be with in a comfortable distance to the rest rooms. All of these physical objects, barriers on campus I had to overcome.

Somehow, in college I had to be more independent, responsible and mature. Plus, I needed to learn to overcome my own personal physical handicap while living on a college campus.

Again, I think the school administrators, teachers, counselors and others did not pick up the ball and set me aside and explain to me all of these upcoming higher education situations and certainly more importantly, to help guide me on a path to be a successful college student.

Maybe my high school grades were too poor to attend college I thought. My parents did not have the money. So college was quickly fading away from me as a plan, goal or even as a dream.

But then I visited with a representative from a community college and we discussed the college requirements, two requirements, there was a twenty dollar admission fee.

The second requirement was, I needed to be a live person. Both of us agreed, I could easily meet those two requirements to be accepted into college, and the physical layout on campus, there were many stair steps but everything was in one building.

We also discussed class scheduling and decided to schedule my classes to allow myself extra time and not be rushing to class. It was exciting to learn that the junior college was all under one roof which was important for me because I would not need to walk outside in the rain, snow and icy days with my crutches.

Within a few days, I mailed in my college application forms and was accepted into college, without discussing this with my parents.

The big situation was the many flights of stairs that I would need to manage daily on campus. And make it to the restroom on time.

Many students seen me struggle going up and down the stairs with my leg braces, crutches and a heavy book bag strapped around my waist. Within a day or so the male students and some professors were assisting me manipulate the stairs. Usually two men, one on each side of me would lift me up by my arm pits carry me up and down the stairs.

This procedure worked very nicely at the junior and then later at my senior college.. There were times I struggled by myself with the stairs but I always used the same procedure that I did with my first stair steps encounter at the local elementary school.

One evening I received a message from Sharon nearly forty-eight later, when I lived in their house during my freshman year in junior college.

And we chatted about all the things Maurice built for me. The chair that allowed me to put my shoes on alone. Then I would no longer need to get up two hours early and ask Den her son, to help me put my socks and shoes on.

And I would get back at my friend's house from college before anyone would get home. And I would drink several glasses of milk and half a cookie jar of homemade cookies every day. I was starved after all day at college.

Sharon drove me to the community college for orientation and we timed how long it took me to get to each class, the bathroom and cafeteria so I could prepare and not be late to class.

Then some of the male students soon offered to carry me up or down stairs and I told them, "Thank you but can I have a rain check in case I need it?". With my two crutches, a book satchel full of heavy college books and my leg braces that weighed forty pounds, I tackled and struggled with a dozen or more flights of stairs daily.

It took me three years at at my junior college to earn my Associate Degree. But I was enjoying college, traveling with the college baseball team as a statistician with Coach Marks. My studying was generally done on the benches on the concourse.

One day the Dean of Students walked past and asked, how my first semester grades were, which were two C's and two B's. Both us us were pleased, with my grades.

For the next five semesters, my grades continued to improve to where I made the Dean's List and was elected into the, "Who's Who among Students in American Junior Colleges 1972-73."

The Dean of Students came up to me and he said, "I am a better man for knowing you." And I will never forget that.

Then the guidance counselor at my junior college mentioned to me, "Once I seen you here for your second semester, there was no doubt in my mind, that you were going to graduate. After struggling with all of these flights of stairs." Unquote.

Then I enrolled at a senior college in January 1977, I was so excited to quit the factory assembly line work where I worked to save money for college, for nearly three years to continue my college dreams. The senior college was much more difficult for me academically and physically.

At SHU my senior college I struggled greatly in my personal growth, trying to find myself. There I began my personal counseling for nearly two years. The counseling quite likely saved my life from depression.

To make this short, I had to come to terms with my Cerebral Palsy and learn to like myself in many different situations.

For the countless unmentioned people in this book, in college, in my life, will forever be a part of my life. And with that, I thank you with all my heart because I would not have graduated from college without all of your help, from every one of you.

Over the years, I remember one of my high school teachers tell me near my high school graduation, "You will never make it in college." His statement is one of the reasons why I did graduate from college, he motivated me. But then the final credits belong to my mother for not giving up on me and Jesus.

The "S" Question

My life experiences was constantly changing as a young adult, experiencing college life in my early twenties was perhaps the most positive change.

The first time living away from my family, maybe not a big deal for most people, unless you are disabled like me. There was so much to learn about myself, living a somewhat sheltered life and so immature, in the shadows of my family. But many new people came into my life and helped inspire me to do my best.

In the spring of 1972, while I jostled near the gymnasium on my crutches at college, one of my classmates walked toward me.

Sometimes he helped carry me up and down the stairs at college But today his shy demeanor was unusual, from his normal outgoing, loud character he showed in our classroom. He always was self-assured with himself.

As he approached me, he put his arm gently across my shoulder and asked with a nervous smile, "Lonnie, please don't get me wrong, but may I ask you a question?"

"Sure go ahead." I wondered.

"Can you have sex?" He asked me frankly, seriously but yet nervously.

"Yes," was my answer but knowing I was still a virgin? Then we went our separate ways.

His question surprised me with his honestly and had me thinking. My friend asked what other people may have wondered.

"Do handicapped people have sex?" His question, had me thinking. Maybe other people had questions about disabled people.

Then I began thinking how could I improve or to change some public myths about disabled people. To help everyone feel more comfortable being around disabled people.

My sexuality issue was a major psychological maturing problem for many years, along with my lack of interacting with and dating women was a troubling self-worthlessness issue for me.

Through my high school and college years, mother always told me, "Just be her friend." But maybe I did not want to be her friend, I wanted a girlfriend and a sexual relationship.

My friends during these years were my most positive aspect in life. But the girl friend issue kept growing and knawing deep inside my psychological being with self-worthlessness and self-hate feelings.

Until my mid-twenties, I still did not have a job, money, car or a driver's license to call a friend to socialize and be comfortable with a woman. With my Cerebral Palsy my dating was only a dream.

In college and Graduate School I struggled greatly in relationships, sexuality and depression. The feeling of worthlessness consumed me. This developed into suicidal thoughts, hating my body and much more.

Another person that touched my mind and heart was a woman in college, I do not remember her name but she was also disabled but she walked without assistance. She was a pretty and friendly, she always smiled and we talked in the hallways.

She wore her short blond hair around her shoulders. Her one eye was crossed and her walking motion was quite different from a normal person. Her left arm looked like a small finger that protruded from her left shoulder.

She carried her dorm keys hooked over her left "finger or arm," among other things tucked under this small limb, against her body.

Now I realize, decades later, in my maturity, what a wonderful person she was. And what a fool I was in not including her as my friend, which might have lasted a lifetime.

Her gentle smile, shyness and kindness showed me that she seemed to be at peace with herself, I admired her and wished I had that kind of peace.

Maybe she wanted a good friend. There was another lost opportunity because of my immaturity. And I want to apologize to her. She showed me her great kindness. With her, I could have been a better person or friend along the way.

Dantrium

Dantrium a new experimental muscle relaxing drug was offered to me in 1972. With the hope in helping my speech and body to relax and function better.

The dantrium was taken over a four week period. During the first week, I took two capsules a day. The second week, I took four capsules a day. The third week, I took six capsules a day. And the fourth of this experiment, I took eight capsules a day of twenty-five mg.

With the increased dosage my muscles throughout my body was more relaxed and less painful. But my body had more strain and difficulty from weakness to keep moving around under the influence the medication.

The speech professor allowed me to give a ten minute speech without the medication on audio tape. Then four weeks later, repeating the same speech on audio tape under the influence of dantrium.

We noticed my speech was much clearer, more understandable on tape and easier to speak with the dantrium. My chest, ribs, jaws, facial muscles, tongue, lips and throat were much more relaxed, so I breathed easier and deeper.

Several years later, without any medication at another college, a friend stopped in my room to visit me. There I sat behind my student desk studying, listening and singing a song from the stereo. When I finished singing, she totally surprised me and said, "You have a very nice voice Lon, when you sing softly."

Her comment was certainly the most rewarding, uplifting positive comment that I have ever received about my voice. Nobody ever said anything like that to me before about my funny distorted, raspy voice. That was a great feeling.

My friend also brought books and research materials so I did not need to struggle several sets of stair steps going to the library.

My Third Leg Surgery

Prior to my junior year at college, I decided to have my third surgery on my legs, this time on my adductor muscles. This surgery everyone hoped would eliminate my knot kneed walking motion.

With every step I took, my knees would rub together and get sore with bloody open blisters on my inside knee joints. And my feet always had the tendency to cross each other.

The surgery took place at a major medical hospital in Indianapolis, in early August 1979. The surgeons and my plans was then returning to college in September. The surgery went well, and I remember setting outside of the hospital, in the hot summer sun with dad. The sun was a great feeling, a break from my gloomy hospital room.

The two incisions were left open, stuffed with medical gauze soaked in Betadine. The doctor wanted my muscles to heal first from the inside out. My testicles felt swollen, like two soft balls were taped to my groin.

The bandage dressing often needed changing on the tendons in my groin area that attached my adductor muscle to my thigh to my pelvic bone.

It was an eerie feeling with the probing of fingers on my tendons and groin tissue inside my body. This was embarrassing and humbling for me when the nurses seen my penis and testicles being exposed.

The recovery was progressing nicely and my parents went back home as I continued my physical therapy.

Secondly, my surgeon was pleased with my progress. So he went on scheduled vacation. But for some reason, there was no doctors monitoring my progress for the next few days.

Things quickly went bad, first I accidentally wet the bed. Then I had infection in my incisions and viral pneumonia.

Many times, I remember awaking up just long enough to see my food tray being delivered to my room. But I fell back asleep, completely missing my meals.

One day during this ordeal, I asked a nurse to help me call my mother and tell her what was going on. The only thing, I remember saying was, "Mom I am very sick. Can you come down?"

During the weekend before I do not remember my parents visiting me, nor do I remember opening up my mail.

Later I wondered, "Who was opening up my mail?" The nurses told me, I opened my own mail, but I did not remember. Nor do I remember setting up in a wheelchair in the hallway eating watermelon, alert and carrying a conversation with dad.

Then one day a nurse walked in my hospital room, joyfully, smiling and she said, "Welcome back Lonnie."

"What do you mean?" I asked her.

"Lonnie, you came very close to dying twice", the nurse looked me into the eyes and stated.

My thought might have been maybe I wanted to die, but for some reason, "Jesus had to be in control, because I certainly did not remember anything."

Then suddenly I had the happiest feeling that I have ever had, simply happy to be alive. Then my thoughts came back to reality, full of pain and helplessness in that hospital bed.

Within a day or two mom came down to help take care of me and make sure that I was eating properly. But the surgeon was still on vacation and mom could not get any helpful answers to our questions on my weaken conditions.

Mom called Ms. Anita S, the only person we knew, within the hospital system, who might be able to find the answers that mother was desperately searching for.

We knew Anita over twenty years, ever since I was five years old and a regular outpatient visitor at the C. P. Clinic, just a couple of buildings away from the this hospital.

Ms. S. was always around the clinic. And I noticed all the medical staff including the doctors took her orders and decisions seriously. Ms. S. was a wonderful person to be on my side. She was always smiling and giving out encouragement to all the other Cerebral Palsy patients, parents and everyone else.

"Hello, Lonnie". Ms. S. surprised me with her big smile as she walked into my hospital room, "Good to see you. Welcome back," she said smiling. "For a while there, you gave all of us a big scare." Then she turned and started listening and talking quietly with my mother, filling us in with more medical details on my conditions.

"Welcome back…a big scare," were two big frightening comments that I could not fully comprehend at the time. But I was still extremely saddened and disappointed in my weakened, painful, helpless physical condition.

Feeling disappointed and realizing that I could not go back to college this fall semester. College had already started two weeks earlier. And I would not be in college for quite some time in my condition.

Somehow, I lost all memory of my daily life for over two weeks with these surgery complications. That was quite frightening having no memory of my life, and nearly dying twice.

The next day, my doctor returned from his vacation. Then we learned my kidneys had stopped functioning, I had viral pneumonia and my temperature was one-hundred and five degrees. The nurses packed my body in ice to bring down my temperature, and monitored my other medical conditions. And I lost nearly twenty pounds in two weeks, my weight was down to eighty pounds.

And I asked my doctor if I could have a beer to help keep my kidneys functioning?

The next morning the nurse brought in my medications. She was tall and very pretty with her strawberry blond hair pinned up on her head. She was about my age, mid-twenties, just recently graduated from nursing school I thought, with no wedding band on her finger.

"Good afternoon, Mr. Shipe," the nurse joyfully greeted me as she quickly walked into my hospital room.

"Hey. Hi," I responded, "did you bring my beer the doctor ordered for me? The beer was to help my kidney's function better,' as we smiled at each other, knowingly she did not buy my lame excuse.

Quickly she leafed through my medical folder, "Yes he did approve a beer, I will get it for you." Within a moment she left my room and returned with a can of beer and proceeded to pour it in a glass. Instantly, the beer foamed over the drinking cup, down on to the eating table and nearly onto my hospital bed.

Silently, I smiled and giggled as she scurried around trying to dry up the spilled beer. Thinking she was not a beer drinker, because she did not know how to pour beer into a glass, without the beer foaming over.

"You owe me another beer," as I smiled trying to coax another beer from her because she wasted half of my beer.

"No, sorry," she said while quickly apologized while she mopped up my spilled beer with a towel, "the doctor only ordered one beer", she continued, almost teasing me.

"Just wait," I thought until my college drinking buddies hear this story. "What a story this will be."

One late afternoon, another nurse maybe in her mid-twenties, possibly a recent nursing graduate entered my room. We began chatting about college and my sadness on missing the fall semester.

Then she added, "If I have some free time, I will try to come back and we can talk a few minutes." she said hurriedly left my room smiling.

That would really be a joy to talk with someone, because I was very depressed on my physical condition and disappointed on not returning to college, I missed my friends tremendously and felt lonely.

In the early evening the nurse returned. Quietly she pushed the chair next to the head of my bed. She sat just inches from me, as I lay in the hospital bed. We quietly talked about my college and future plans.

She asked me a few questions about my family. It was a nice conversation about fifteen minutes or so, then we paused a moments and she asked me if I had a girlfriend.

Honestly, I told her, I did not have a girlfriend and I never been in a dating relationship. She encouraged me, in her very enjoyable brief conversation to keep trying and then she left wishing me well, I was so happy she visited me.

Gayle and My Self Worth

My physical therapy had progressed enough for me to attempt my first post-surgery steps before leaving the hospital. This was a new experience for me to be using my crutches right after surgery.

With my previous two leg surgeries I spent months in casts, then regaining my strength and learning to walk all over again with my crutches and braces.

For a few days Gayle and I have been friendly chatting with each other in the hospital halls, while she visited her father. She was in her mid-twenties.

One afternoon, she secretly placed a letter on my hospital bed stand. Her twelve or more page letter shared how she, wished she could be here to watch me take my first post-surgery steps with my crutches.

Gayle's letter was a pleasant surprise, she was the first woman to write me. The letter was not a "love letter" but she showed more thoughts and feelings than just, "it was a nice pleasure to meet you" letter.

A few months after my surgery and a few letters to each other, Gayle and I did have a dinner date, we danced a few times and we had a nice evening.

After our date, I am not sure why, other than I was truly scared, insecure with my cerebral palsy, immaturity or some other sub-conscious psychological reason. But I did not follow through with something that I dearly needed and wanted. And that was a girlfriend, a companion, including a sexual relationship with a woman.

One Saturday, Gayle's friend dropped her off at the motel in a local town and her friend picked Gayle up the next morning. This was a safe place for Gayle, after all I could not take her to mom's house just yet.

There were no plans on a sexual relationship, other than my thoughts but I was hopeful for a sexual relationship.

In my heart if a sexual relationship happened, the first initial move would need to come from Gayle, I was so insecure and scared with my cerebral palsy. Reflecting back, Gayle likely did make the first move by leaving the motel door open and the light on, as I looked into the rear view mirror and continued to drive away.

Thinking Gayle had good intentions on developing a boy-girlfriend relationship. Again, I was scared to death, weak, to make the first move for a sexual relationship.

Being laughed at, rejected and my psychological feelings of worthlessness haunted me from my past. What a big, lousy coward, I was at that moment. Actually, I hated myself for many years over this, on being such a coward.

It does not help my psychological feeling and self-worth when someone adds, I did the right thing by not entering that motel room.

And I was dearly afraid of an unwanted pregnancy. And worse, I might have felt not worthy of a girlfriend or lover. Fearful of being ridiculed, and laughed at, not by Gayle, but my own thoughts of helplessness and worthlessness.

Afraid, perhaps, unconsciously, that I was somehow putting my mother's face on each woman that I wanted to get involved with. Those unconscious thought were brought out through counseling later on in my life.

Mother always told me when I became interested in dating someone, "just be her friend." But I did not want to always be a friend, I wanted a boy and girlfriend relationship, including sex.

During my late teens and through the next decade of my life, I was extremely lonely. In my mid-twenties was the time I began to think about suicide.

It took a couple of more years when I learned that I was "OK, no matter what," through my counseling sessions. And I also learned more about my self-worth, my maturing and the negative connotations of placing my mother's face on every woman that I was interested in.

My dad's silly, joking comment that he, "wanted the first date to see if the woman was good enough for you," was raging in my mind also. This hurt me deeply. Thinking I was, not good enough for anyone's love.

During my therapy with Bernie, she helped me to realize with each and every relationship with women that I pursued, I would most likely fail, as I have before.

Or I would end up hurting myself even more, if I did not learn to work through these issues of women, my self-worth and my issues with my parents that I had psychologically negatively planted into my subconscious thinking.

My worthless, guilty feelings if my body did not cooperate and perform as a woman might have expected, with the Cerebral Palsy. It was not a gentleman issue but a fear issue. All of these thoughts and issues I had to do deal with, Am I worthy of this relationship and the continuous circle of my low self- esteem and putting my mother's face on Gayle's face and separating the two faces, the two women.

Dad's laughter, his comments, mother's face, my weak bladder all subconsciously fell in line as I drove away leaving Gayle there alone in the motel room. Oh I hated myself, I hate this body, I wished I was dead.

Bernie worked with me through my therapy sessions on other issues, "Why are you interested in woman that look like your mother?" She asked and added, "Why do you choose women that end up hurting you?"

For the first time in my life, I suddenly realized like a bolt of lightning flashing before my eyes with those two questions, "Bernie was so right."

Bernie raised another issue, "Stop putting your mother's face on every woman that you want a relationship with."

Then Bernie wanted me to mentally set my mother there on the bed in my dorm room and tell her, "Mom, I want to have a sexual relationship with a woman."

This was so painful and very difficult for me to do. My throat went dry, I was having trouble breathing and I was almost crying. But I needed to fight and work through this, because this subconscious psychological battle and war within myself was slowly filling me with more worthlessness, guilt and self-hate between the women, mother and myself.

"Tell your mother again," Bernie said more loudly and sternly. "Tell your mother again, you want to have a sexual relationship with a woman."

"Mom, I want to have a sexual relationship with a woman", I stated quite firmly and by this time I was emotionally drained and my tears were running down my cheeks.

And I told my mom in my imagination, as if she was setting on my dorm room bed over and over, until it was not quite so difficult and hard for me to say. But I also felt a tremendous release of pressure and quilt that had been inside of me for maybe over a decade.

This was something that I had to do, to work through this process of not put my mother's face on every woman that I was interested in dating.

So I had to separate myself from my parents, one way I could easily do this was keep going to college and stay away from home.

Over two years, in the late seventies I had thoughts of suicide, I did not like myself, I hated my weak bladder, my disabled body, along with my "you talk funny" speech "what good am I?"

My lack of confidence, immaturity, much deeper intense psychological thoughts all needed changing with therapy, to change my life around.

My therapy would not be an ending to my psychological issues with women, but only a new beginning down a long difficult road to hopefully gain peace, respect and confidence with myself.

There were still many unhealthy psychological feelings on "not liking myself" to be dealt with, along with other unconscious, hidden, hateful, psychological feelings all directed at myself. Although I still believed I was a good person but not who I wanted to become with peace within myself.

These emotional issues I had to learn to separate my mother's face, other people's words, comments and other things from my psychological feelings, so I could continue on with living my life for myself. Before I could feel comfortable enough to be in a relationship with a woman, I needed to be comfortable with my handicap, physically and psychologically.

Bernie wondered and asked, "When you had the accident with your parents car was that a suicidal act?" We both agreed, it might have been.

From my teenage years until I became engaged to Eugenia at the age of thirty-one, there were very few positive situations with any interaction with a woman for more than a one-time date or just a college social gathering.

A gentleman's courtesy I could not do, such as holding a woman's hand while she walks up and down steps. I, going up and down steps by myself was often impossible. Helping her with her coat or opening the doors for her, on and on. All of these things I wanted to do in my mind but my body would not cooperate.

Thinking about or not pursuing a relationship with a woman certainly had a major part with my body, my speech, low esteem and I blamed my stupid body with cerebral palsy.

Looking back over these issues, I was not strong enough to realize or understand to see through my issues of loneliness and self-worth and see the good that I had within myself that Jesus created.

When I was not successful at something such as, getting up after I fell down, making it to the restroom on time, doing better in school or relating with women, I did not like myself, I was not good enough for anything I thought.

Fortunately, God blessed me with a vision of "HOPE." Sometimes hope was all I had. And Jesus blessed me with a great family and a tremendous supporting cast of "friends" throughout my life.

Because, "can't never did anything" as mom told me thousands of times. There was "HOPE" at least most of the time in my mind.

There were other things that needed to be added to my personality, work around things, work as hard and as long as one can, improvise, keep learning, improving and never give in but perhaps take another route.

Also through counseling I learned that I needed to, "be good to myself." If I would have had more self-confidence or greater self-esteem, my life might have been a great deal better and easier, not only for myself but for my family also.

Bernie helped me work through many other psychological issues. She has my ultimate respect and admiration for "listening to me "and helping me along my way.

There were serious actual moments of self-worthlessness, self-hate and suicidal thoughts inside of me subconsciously and consciously for several years during the nineteen seventies as a young adult. Today, I am alive from the help of Bernie in the late 1970's and of course with the help of my friends and Jesus.

Diamond Ring

My last undergraduate class, was a values class with the theme on how people treat others. It took me several weeks to decide what project to come up with, on how people were treated differently and viewed. But my whole life I observed and learned how people interacted with me.

Rarely, did I take charge as a student with assertiveness in discussions, because I did not like my "funny voice." So I sat quietly listening to the professor and other students for several weeks but I knew class participation is important and I knew the sooner I spoke up in class or participated the better it would be for me.

But I had this great fear of saying something stupid and being laughed at, being misunderstood or unable to speak clearly. Over the years, no collective group of people ever laughed at me when I was speaking within a serious discussion. In almost every situation, as difficult as it was for me to speak clearly, people truly listened to me.

To hold people's attention, to the point where I could feel every person's eyes were directed at me. The power at times, to draw people into me and everyone trying hard to give me their total concentration, to not only listen but to hear what I was trying to say, with my "funny voice" was an awesome experience for me.

Speaking in a classroom with other students all revolved on relaxing so I could speak clearly. Sometimes, if I was suddenly, unexpectedly called upon to answer a question, my speech would be better or I could quite possibly be unable to speak at all. There I would set in a classroom and fret and be thinking, "I hope I am not called upon." A one or two word answer to a question I was much more comfortable with.

One evening, I approached Kathy, a classmate and I shared with her my thoughts of us working on a class project together.

The project was about me, a disabled man, with a non-disabled girlfriend, shopping for an engagement ring and observing how the retailer interacted with us. Kathy thought that was a great idea.

Later that week, we visited a jewelry store in the local mall. We did not walk together holding hands, as many boy and girlfriends do while shopping for engagement rings. Because I needed to hold onto my crutches but we walked closely together.

Cautiously, I was very care full with my crooked steps, as my toe plated shoes scraped on the mall's concourse tiled floor. Surely, I did not want to slip or lose my balance and fall down in front of everyone at the shopping mall.

On our short trek, we entered the jewelry store. Within a few feet after entering the store, we sat on two chairs next to the diamond ring counter. Kathy and I sat side by side just a few inches away from each other.

"May I help you?" the salesman asked quickly from behind the counter.

"Yes', I said, 'we would like to look at some diamond rings please." Immediately the clerk picked out a diamond ring and set the boxed ring on the glass counter top, in front of Kathy.

"This diamond is very pretty", as the clerk spoke more directly toward Kathy, while picking out a diamond ring and handing the ring to Kathy.

Upon receiving the ring, Kathy was smiling and she turned a bit toward me as she placed the ring on her left ring finger. Both of us were smiling and agreeing the diamond was beautiful.

Then we began looking at other rings underneath the glass encased counter. With every ring exchange the salesman presented Kathy the rings, then Kathy shared with me. We were interested and excited as we talked, giggling and looking at each ring.

An important part of our project was observing how the salesman interacted with a woman becoming engaged to a handicapped man. And how the salesman interacted with a disabled man looking for an engagement ring.

The salesman nicely greeted us from the very beginning but he never shook either of our hands, and he quickly fell into our suspected outcome by never personally interacting with me.

All of his comments and questions during his presentation were directed toward Kathy and he rarely looked at me. He was basically leaving me out of his presentation and all of his attention was toward Kathy, as we suspected.

"I prefer gold bands instead of sterling silver. And I would like to see a larger carat," I said while thinking about how little I know about jewelry. This was our project and I wanted to be involved in the conversation but I spoke relaxed and clearly.

It was a nice interesting, fun, few moments, in role playing with Kathy. She rolled the diamond ring back and forth, moving her arm and hand around in front of us, observing the diamond as it glistened on her finger.

Kathy and I played our roles well. The salesman's only interaction with me, was when he presented the diamond rings to my classmate that I requested. After a few more minutes of looking at the rings we decided not to purchase a ring or put a ring on layaway, as the salesman asked.

Soon we were leaving the jewelry store, back toward campus discussing our event. Then I should have "use your head" as mother often reminded me. This was a perfect opportunity to ask Kathy if she had time for dinner or a glass of wine before returning to campus. But I did not "use my head," for a continuation of a nice evening and good conversation with Kathy.

Yet again, maybe the subconscious thoughts from my mother "just be her friend." Or from my dad when he often said to me in a jokingly manner, "I get the first date."

Sure I had a few nice dates, every few years but I never had two dates with the same woman. And the couple of dates that I did have were with nice, pretty women too.

Being a gentleman is very important to me and I could not do what I wanted or fill that role. That bothered me a great deal I was not able to measure up to my own self standards of being a man, a gentlemen, because of my Cerebral Palsy.

Within a day or two back in the classroom, we were ready to share our experience with the jewelry salesman with our classmates.

For the first time, in class Kathy and I sat side by side each other. Soon after our class period began, Kathy was sharing our project and developments with thirty or so other colleagues.

Everything went well for her and there was some interaction with the Professor. At this moment, I still did not say anything or interject my thoughts to support Kathy's input to our project.

And I knew, with all my heart, to the best of my speaking ability, with the powerful fear that I have of speaking in class, my heart was pounding, my fingers gripping tightly onto my desktop.

My throat was dry but I swallowed hard, took a deep breath and said, "I have something to add to Kathy's comments," while raising my one hand to get the Professor's attention.

After I began speaking a few words, remembering to breathe and to relax my lips and jaws, speaking just became much easier for me. Most people on campus have heard me talk before.

With my colleagues I started sharing and reinforcing Kathy's statements and also added how the salesman started out by ignoring me and each ring I handled came from Kathy and not from the salesman.

Each breath I took and every word that I shared in the classroom was very difficult to force out of my mouth to say loudly and clearly. But soon every word spoken just became a bit easier to say.

Consciously relaxing my face, lips, tongue, arms and chest to breathe easier, improves my speaking tremendously. And I realize this, but because of my Cerebral Palsy speaking is often very difficult or impossible.

Psychologically, if I can block out all other people and try to put myself on a one on one conversation, speaking in a group becomes a bit easier sometimes.

And I am so blessed and fortunate to be able to experience so many of life's normal activities.

But I think it is my responsibility to teach or help other individuals to feel comfortable in dealing with or being around handicapped people.

Teaching people in the normal world, that handicapped people have the same dreams, hopes, feelings, needs and desires that every other normal person has. Perhaps, this is my responsibility to the general public, educational and medical field on a national and or international stage.

Unfortunately, perhaps many handicapped people do not get to experience the things that are important to themselves.

More Trouble with My Hands

Never was I able to turn my hands palms up. The muscles and tendons were too short or too tight to do that wrist function. If I wanted to hand something to someone, I needed to place the object into the other person's palm.

And people could not put objects into my hands I needed to take things from their hands. Plus, I could not put my wallet in my hip pocket or do anything behind my back with my hands.

During the mid-nineteen-seventies I could do a normal handshake, but then the pain and tightness began in my right arm, hand and fingers. Then I began going to doctors and Chiropractor's for several years.

Those fancy handshakes the athletes and other people do caught my attention and how nice it would be able to have the muscular freedom to do those handshakes.

Nothing really helped my body to feel comfortable in just moving about. My body was not part of who I wanted to become, I felt that my body had betrayed me somehow.

The pain, restrictions, the bondage never left my body even with medications. And I became discouraged and quit visiting doctors for my neck and arm problems for many years.

Everybody could quickly tell that I was disabled by my movements and mobility, including my hands and fingers restrictions. If you watch a normal person's movement, it looks more fluid, more easily done.

My physical body actions were more difficult, restrained, slow motion and jerky. My body moved in a mechanical, robotic way, it seemed to me much different in real time body movements.

One summer morning of maybe 2012, I woke up and feeling much more so, that my body was not normally functioning the way I thought it should. This seemed silly, after all these years living with Cerebral Palsy and my C-6 spinal cord fracture that caused numbness, tingling, weakness and non-functioning ability.

Both of my neck surgeries we performed by my neurosurgeon. His goals were to stop the tingling sensations in my hands and fingers and have the capability to shake hands in a normal gentlemanly way, without pain or stiffness.

Then I learned as a middle aged adult that my brain looked "normal" on the CT scan. This news was surprising because all along in my life I was told and I believed that I had brain damage since my birth and was expecting the CT scan to verify my thoughts.

Now I am wondering what really did happen to my brain and my head at birth. Maybe the forceps did damage my head. Perhaps my real issue was during my birthing process. At some moment, in a young age, I was told my brain did not receive enough oxygen during my birthing, which I will never understand.

The only time I was able to bend over while setting on my bed or a low stool and tie my own shoe strings was in my early twenties.

It took a great effort to play tricks between my mind and body to get my body to cooperate with my mind. Often that trick was to get my mind away from the struggle of my body.

One of these tricks I learned from a doctor at the C. P. Clinic. The doctor was trying to bend my legs at my knees but my spastic, tight muscles were resisting the doctor's efforts.

The doctor starting saying things like, ice cream, pop-cycle or other kinds of food to distract my mind and bend my knees, at the same time by applying gentle pressure on my legs to get my knees to bend more freely.

And I tried the doctor's technique to get my hips, knees and ankles to bend for me, sometimes it did not work. Wiggling and tricking my body into a particular position, was the only way to tie my own shoe strings. It was embarrassing for me to ask other people to tie my shoe strings.

Swallowing is another issue after my first neck surgery, the problem with swallowing and choking. My reasoning is, my throat was pulled to one side, so the doctor could repair my C-4, C-5, and C-6 vertebras.

In my view, now my throat is not quite normal, so I choke more often. People keep saying eat slowly and chew my food but most of the time; I believe the choking is not my fault. Often I feel like I am choking when I simply swallowing my saliva.

Many people, including my mother said my voice is a bit more understandable after my surgery. Before surgery we were informed that I might not be able to talk for three months after surgery but I was talking normally within a few hours after surgery.

The neurosurgeon and everyone thought that was amazing to be talking so soon after surgery but in my mind there was a logical reason and that was a miracle from Jesus Christ.

"Tie my shoes," I heard often from other residents that lived in the dorm. They heard that phrase from me asking them to tie my shoes. It was alright when some friends kept saying "tie my shoes" as they passed my dorm room, they were just joking with me. But it was a little embarrassing to ask people to tie my shoes. When untying my shoes I used my crutches, to untie the shoestrings.

The men that lived in "Moose Hall" were the ones that rushed into my dorm room when the fire alarms were screaming over the P.A. system, to get me up, dressed and outside in a matter of a few seconds. These guys were fantastic with their helpfulness along with many others who helped make my college experiences, a lifelong, great memory.

Feeding myself and cutting the food up I did well but I could not cradle silverware between my thumbs or forefingers and eat. The spoon or fork is gripped with my palms down and usually with my right hand.

And I could not insert a belt through the belt loops in the slacks while wearing the clothing. Before I put the slacks on, I inserted the belt through the belt loops first. It is impossible to put my arms and hands behind my back to put the belt on. It amazed me how dad could be completely dressed in thirty-seconds it seemed.

We search for our own identity, to stand out within a crowd but in other ways we want to be like everyone else. It took me years to learn and accept some things about myself, knowing I was different but somewhat the same as everyone else and to learn that, "I was still okay, no matter what."

Being an athlete at heart, I enjoyed watching the athletes and other people do all of their fancy, interesting handshakes. But I could not do those simple acts. Psychologically it is a big deal to do what you want to do.

Nothing really helped my body to feel comfortable in moving about. My body was not part of who I was on the inside I believed my body had betrayed me.

My shoulders and arms I depended a great deal on, with little cooperation from in my legs to move around. With every step I took my body was totally kept in balance with my crutches, shoulders, arms, hands and fingers.

When I fell and broke my neck in the bathroom, I lost the strength in my whole body and the ability to function normally even with my cerebral palsy. But I had good sensation everywhere but not in my hands and fingers.

Shaving is another task that changed after my spinal cord fracture. Shaving is much harder and done totally right handed. Small things were difficult to distinguish by touch without looking at the object.

We needed to quickly come up with a good plan for me to handle my urinal better. Hooking the urinal over the wheelchair frame brought us closer to a solution of keeping my urinal handy but it was a long ways from me being comfortable.

And I could not handle buttons or zippers, and I needed a workable procedure to keep my penis out in the open and cover myself up by using a lap towel and to keep that from blowing away outside. Things need to be shared, no matter how embarrassing they are, if we are to help other people.

We learned new procedures in handling the urinal to help keep myself from wetting my pants several times daily but accidents happen. Condom catheters did not work well for me.

One windy day, I was outside in my electric wheelchair and suddenly the wind blew the urinal off my wheelchair frame and it landed on the street.

Now I use a cord around my neck to carry the urinal by my side at all times because of my weak bladder. But sometimes the urinal does slip off the cord onto the floor or street, when this happens I take the cord off of my neck and dangle the cord down to hook the urinal handle and pick up the urinal myself.

We must not give up just because things do not work out well. Somehow we must fight, search and find a solution to all of our needs and dreams. There is no joy in wetting my pants.

At the end of the day wet or dry, Eugenia lifts me up in the hoist, cleans me up for bed then she tosses the clothes into the clothes washer. Why worry about it, both of us do the best we can but I wish I could do better.

It is easy to say, "That is the way it is", but we must not get caught up in this situation but we must do our best but I pray for peace of mind. Someday Jesus will make everything perfect.

Three Great Friends Doug, Terry and Larry

It has been nearly twenty years since I last seen Doug, I hardly recognized him at dad's funeral in December 1988. Dad was in the hospital only two days before he passed. His autopsy indicated he died from a "burst aorta in his chest," at the age of fifty-five.

As I turned I seen a tall man with red graying hair, and I asked, "Who are you?" If I was not so surprised to see him, I might have recognized this person.

Doug was my first great friend and our families were friends. We always played together when we were growing up. In grade school Doug already had great athletic skills and talent. Everything seemed so easy for him, school, running and playing with me. His body motion was so fluid, strong, and quick. Everything that Doug could do, I wanted to do.

Doug taught me so much in life by playing outside sports and games with me and that I could compete too. He played much different with me than he played with normal children. The rules of our games were different too.

Our games, as youngsters were usually outside in front of the big white barn on Maurice's farm. The barn was our backstop and blocked our pitches, so we could retrieve the pitched ball easily when we played wiffle ball. The outfield was the yard and driveway. And the bases were anything we could find, a rag, a stone from the flower bed or lawn chair.

While standing and leaning on my crutches I gripped my left crutch tightly at the hand grip for balance and stability and swing the plastic bat with my right arm.

Doug pitched under handed to me, while standing about fifteen feet away. His game was not about striking me out but for fun.

He taught me to stand on my crutches and "swing at the bat," he would always say. The bat was a small yellow, light, plastic wiffle bat.

My swings often miss the ball and sometimes I would fall down on the gravel driveway and skin up my knuckles and get my pants dirty. But I did not care, I was still playing "baseball" with my friend having a great time. Our parents would yell at us to not play so hard and be careful, but I could not wait for Doug to make his next pitch to me.

Basketball was more difficult for me but I enjoyed holding up my crutch high over my head trying to block one of Doug's shots, but he could move and I could not, yet it was fun trying.

"Running" to the bases when I did get a "hit," was just a crooked, jerky motion or I would fall down from trying to go to fast. Running was just my dream for my whole life.

My hits would only go about thirty feet or so across the yard. Doug could easily smack the ball above the tall tree tops in the yard.

Pitching the ball over home plate was difficult, I could only toss a ball maybe ten feet and rarely did I throw a strike to Doug, while leaning on my crutches.

Many times Doug caught the ball in his hands before the ball went to the backstop. If I happened to make a decent pitch Doug would smack the ball, then he would retrieve the ball after he circled the bases for a home run. But I did not care I was still playing ball with my best friend. He never made excuses and never allowed me to make excuses. Yes, I just wanted to be like him to run, play sports with integrity and talent.

Doug was more than just my best boyhood friend, he was the person that I wanted to be. Maybe he was my idol. He had the freedom of movement and the athletic skills that I could only dream about.

We rarely seen each other after our grade school years, our families had separate busy lives. Doug was a good athlete in high school, and he played baseball and basketball. During Doug's collegiate career he played baseball, in the early 1970's.

But there were no amount of miles that could diminish my love, friendship and respect for Doug. These feelings are truly mutual both of us.

Then I turned around at my dad's funeral in December 1988 and there stood Doug, standing quietly behind me. It was a shock and a flood of emotions so I did not recognize him in a flash, and with that I was a bit embarrassed. But oh, I was so happy to see him.

Doug knew that, I was having problems with pain in my arms. Little did I know then it was a spinal cord problem in my neck.

He knew and shared with me that I have lived my whole life with pain and indignity. And that I learned to cope with all kinds of problems and survived the physical pain. Only a best friend would have those memories.

Doug believed that I was "one brave person!" He remembered my leg surgeries and the weeks and in some cases months, that I had to spend with casts from my toes to hips, and or from my toes to my arm pits. He shared how my tears and pain hurt him so much. It hurt Doug to see me in pain.

In my own way Doug shared that I was an inspiration, an influence to him in our younger years. Doug knew that I had every reason not to live, not to walk, not to succeed. And I was told I would never walk, make it through school or not live very long. Then proving all the professionals wrong, this was somehow Doug's inspiration from me. Who am I to disagree with his feeling. But I do agree, our feeling are mutual for each other in our own personal ways.

It was a joy to play pool, wiffle ball, kick ball and everything else with all my heart and soul. And I believed that I could compete. Yes, perhaps the rules were bent a little bit. The fear that I never showed. And when, I fell down I needed to get back up. If I swung and missed I would want to try again. After all, how could I be like my best friend, even in heart and desire if I did not keep on trying.

Doug had some talent that God gave him. But according to Doug, I taught him how to use a little bit of talent and a whole lot of heart and soul to become successful.

You know some athletes got nervous before a game. They are nervous because they are doubtful about their abilities. Doug said, honestly he was never that way before a game. He only wanted to compete and get up if he was knocked down, maybe he got that from me.

After he learned his lessons from me he said, it added confidence to all of his endeavors. He never had any fear to try something. Doug learned from me, a valuable lesson of life, to never give up, no matter what.

Unfortunately, I never seen Doug play competitive sports in high school or college. But I did set in my bedroom in March 1970 and listened to the play-by-play broadcast on my old battery operated radio, listening as Doug playing on his high school varsity basketball team during the Michigan High School Basketball Sectional. Wishing I was there watching him and rooting him on to victory.

Doug and dad were two of the most athletic skilled people that I knew in my life. Dad's athletic genes I believe are locked up and restricted by bondage in my body with Cerebral Palsy.

This is the only explanation I have explaining my athletic skills. These athletic skills lived within me in spite of my Cerebral Palsy. My "hoop", my "home plate", and playing "catch" with grandpa proved to me that "some great athletic skills" along with my mental desire lived deeply, trapped within my brain and body.

The nearest I ever came to participating in basketball was when dad's friend made me a special "hoop" for me when I was in grade school. The "hoop" made of a thin band of steel hooked over my bedroom door.

Mom bought me a real basketball net, so I could hang the basketball net onto the "hoop." A real official size basketball was too large and heavy for me so I played with a lightweight inflated ball as my "basketball" so nothing would break in my bedroom.

My "hoop" was about five feet above the floor. The only way I could "shoot baskets" was while I was on my knees. With some imagination, while playing "basketball" by myself, I could shoot free throws or make a last second shot to win the basketball game.

Basketball for me was played like this for hours on the weekends and during the summer for many years. With a little imagination and a lot of joy, this was my sport also.

Into my mid-teens, the hoop still hung on my bedroom closet door. Then I took a piece of cord and tied the bottom loops of the basketball net together, so when the ball passed through the hoop the basketball would still remain in the net. Then I would not need to chase the ball across the bedroom after every shot.

Yet the ball could easily be pulled through the net. Often I played "basketball" while standing and leaning against an old desk next to my closet, so I could be standing up without my crutches.

With the hoop within approximately twelve inches from my face I could pretend that I was seven feet tall basketball player grabbing the rebounds and dunking the basketball, or making the last second tip in, winning the game. And knowing if I leaned too far or moved too much I would fall flat on my face on the bedroom floor.

Terry and Doug are two friends and athletes that I really enjoyed among others. Terry and I became friends in the seventh grade, I seen the same athletic skills, friendship, joy of living, respect and integrity in Terry through our high school years, that I see in Doug.

Maybe it was not in God's plans for me to play sports like Doug and Terry. But I can believe, if Terry and I had been athletes together, we would have made each other better athlete and greater friends.

Both Terry and Doug certainly made me a better person today because I just wanted to be like "Terry and Doug." They were the athletes and the men that I wanted to be. So I thank both of you for being the friends, men and athletes, that I still admire today.

With the capability of social media Terry and I have reconnected several decades after our high school years. One evening we were posting on social media and Terry encouraged me to keep writing.

He used a football analogy in conjunction with my writing frustrations and scoring a touchdown in a football game.

Terry wanted me to hang in there with my writing, like it was fourth and goal with five seconds to go in the game. And my number was called in the play, to take it in and score the touchdown.

He gave me the confidence in my imagination to score a touchdown. But in reality, Terry was encouraging me to regained my confidence and continue writing. But I needed to do better and also score the two point conversion. My book needed to be published with the hope of helping others around the world.

This was a very inspirational moment, a reminder for me from Terry to keep writing. It does not matter how things are looking or going.

When the pressure is on or when things may not be going well, we must not only keep on going but keep on going with the attitude nothing is going to stop us or beat us, be a winner, be successful, we are okay, no matter what.

Then there is Larry, my friend since the seventh grade, and my best friend since then. Larry told me after we graduated from high school he struggled with reading and he thought he had, "dyslexia." Maybe back then dyslexia was not well known.

So I could relate with Larry's education struggles. Larry was also a great athlete in football and shot putt. During our senior year he was striving to set a school record in shot put.

After I learned to drive and bought myself a car at the age of twenty-five, Larry and I often would set around his house and we would just talk. Sometimes, we went to town and talked some more.

Like Doug and Terry I could only dream of Larry's athletic ability. Through my dreams, I wanted to be like them and my dad. Where I had control of my body and compete in athletics.

Larry has been my best friend and brother for life.

Phil and Jack

Another one of God's Angels in my life was Phil. He helped write and advice President Ronald Reagan on the "American Disabilities Act in 1990", while he was in the United States Army.

Phil would visit me when possible, but cancer took his life, which cut short our tremendous friendship.

Both of us have gone through depression, anger and self-doubts. And on rare occasions self-destructive thoughts. This may be a normal reaction to Phil's cancer and Parkinson Disease. Just as my depression and self-worth denials could also be a product of my circumstances with cerebral palsy and the spinal cord injury.

However, Phil reminded me on one of his visits, that each of us has special gifts. And he shared that he was amazed on my smile and some people that have challenges have never learned to smile, but withdraw into themselves. Thereby depriving ourselves and the world of a universal signal of friendship and language, a smile.

Phil and I had some rough times. We always will until life ends here on earth, and we get into Heaven. But in the meantime, we must find or have a kind, loving spirit and a good mind to put our strengths to work as a goodwill ambassador.

From home, I was reminded that I could write emails, press releases and post on social websites, call people on the telephone or write a book in the privacy of my home. All it takes is time and a kind heart. And Phil genuinely shared with me that I had plenty of both

Phil encouraged me, to pick up my spirits and be assured that he and others cared and loved me. He believed that people are waiting to see my smile and hear my words of encouragement.

It should be much easier for non-challenged people to do this type of God's work. But few people take the time. Whatever our difficulties are, we should not let that stop us. Phil suggested for me to take time and share my kind spirit and God's love with others. Phil will never be forgotten.

Another person Jack, from church who visited me almost every week for over a decade beginning in 1995, after I fell and broke my neck, He listened. We shared and then we prayed. Jack was my bright spot for our weekly visits for an hour or so for nearly two decades, until he was called to Heaven after a heart attack.

What great, wonder friends and mentors Phil and Jack were. If I had mentors like them from junior high through college, my life still would have been difficult. But with them or others, my life would have been much more pleasant and peaceful too.

Jesus brought our lives together for a purpose. That purpose I believe was to brighten our lives with one another for however long each of us lives.

One day I called Phil while he was ill and bed fast with cancer. It was a joy listening to his wisdom on life. The last time we talked Phil's voice was weak and frail but very uplifting in his positive attitude and encouragement.

We were friends for a short time in life but Phil will be a man of courage and compassion with Jesus in his heart. As long as I have a good mind Phil will forever be in my mind and heart. Phil is in Heaven now, with no pain and a new body, I will see him there. Praise the Lord.

My Last Letter to Mother

Dear Mom,

I just need to say "Thank you for everything mom. And I love you with all my heart." You had an added tremendous responsibility as a young mother taking care of and raising me. You did a great, tremendous, fantastic job too. Thank you.

Hopefully the medical profession learned something from both of us, in our successes and accomplishments. Over fifty years ago, the hospitals and the clinics was a tremendous help for us. But you were the true main person in my power, my strength of my future and life along with Jesus.

You probably did not have much support when I was a born or throughout my life. Most likely I was a unique situation to most people back then, including the professional medical system and support group.

You continued on doing your best with each situation for us kids. And I thank God for you and I thank you also mom.

You proved to everyone with the love in your heart you did your best, it showed with every moment of my life with your added responsibility on raising me. You never gave in. You never quit. You taught me how to, "Never Quit," and "Can't Never Did Anything."

Jesus gave you this talent, skill, knowledge and motherhood instinct to take care of me and raise me with our situation. Just believe in your heart, Jesus will reward you beyond our imaginations. He will not leave us.

And I graduated from high school, college then Graduate School because of what you gave me as a child. But I was not that smart perhaps but most of my accomplishments are because of you. I just, "never quit."

And I thank you with all my heart for this "trait" that you gave me on "Never quitting. Never give up." Surely, Jesus gave this blessing to both of us.

Very few people can understand or relate to my "journey" of life and accomplishments, dreams and goals but you can. They never wore my shoes. But you were with me, every step of the way.

Life, for others, might have been a bit easier. My life was certainly given a different path and journey from Jesus, than most everyone.

All the mountains, dead ends, road blocks, wrong way routes that I encountered, including the "society and physical obstacles" along my journey, I overcome because of you.

We worked together around all these obstacles. You taught me how as a youngster and as a man if things do not work out, "never quit, try a different way."

And I had tremendous help all along my life from countless people because these people seen you. People see my mother in my heart, because I "Never Quit because YOU NEVER QUIT" on me.

We thank you dearly. Eugenia, Alexis and I love you with all our hearts.

With Love from the Three of US, Lonnie, Eugenia and Alexis

April 9, 2010.

The Last Time I Seen Mother

Mother was diagnosed with Leukemia around March 2010, and then she passed into Heaven three months later in June.

Mother always did her very best taking care of us three kids. She did everything for me while I was growing up as a child. Now she needed help and there was nothing I could do to help her except pray.

Upon learning that mom had cancer the feeling of helplessness suddenly engulfed me, not that I could cure her cancer but I just wanted to help her in some way. Every day I called her for about a week, then mom said, "Lon, you do not need to call me every day."

One Saturday in June, the three of us, with the help of two other people we went to visit mom.

Our friends struggled greatly in transferring me from in and out of the van into my manual wheelchair and up the five steps into mother's house.

Once in the living room "in my spot" is where everyone decided to set the manual wheelchair. From that view I could still see just about everywhere.

My sister went to get mom from her bedroom. The atmosphere for each of us was very heavy. It was impossible to say anything or look at anyone. The fear of seeing a tear in someone's eyes which would have been my breaking point of "losing it" and crying. My breathing was difficult from the emotional heavy feelings within my heart.

Mom walked very slowly toward us, as my sister held mom's arm. She looked very frail with her white short hair, which use to be brown. But mother had a smile on her face as she walked toward me as I sat unable to move in the wheelchair. Then we gently hugged and kissed each other.

Thinking as mother slowly walked feebly toward me, "I should be the one helping her walk." But I could not help her in any manner other than just being there. The psychological emotional pressure was pressing heavily on my body, chest and heart with the feeling of helplessness. Again, I needed to keep looking at mom and not at anyone else or I would break down crying.

Someone rolled me against the living room wall, maybe fifteen feet from the living room couch. Mother was resting there, wearing her pajamas. All of us were visiting with one another. But soon everyone else went into the kitchen to prepare lunch.

Mom and I were left alone and we talked the best we could being separated into different parts of the room.

"I am so happy all of you came to visit today, I wanted to see you, Eugenia and Alexis," mom said. Her comment brought up another lump in my throat and I swallowed hard to keep my composure.

Mother added, in her weak, soft voice laying on the room couch, "When it is time, let Alexis go." Mom knew Alexis was now a young adult and trying hard to fit in with our lives and yet searching to find her own unique path in life.

At times, I could not hear mother well, and there I sat in the wheelchair in the same room but I needed to be closer to mother, to hold her hand, for at least one last time.

After all these years mom did so much for me and I felt so helpless that I could not roll the wheelchair to be near her, to listen to her or comfort her in any manner, oh I felt so bad.

Then mother spoke up and she said, "My time is very short. I love you very much."

"Mom I love you very much' trying to swallow another big heavy lump, still lodged in my throat and fighting my tears, 'I think you did a fantastic job raising us three kids and especially with me."

Eugenia brought her special Filipina dishes of food, fried rice and egg rolls which everyone loved to eat.

Eugenia asked mom several times if she wanted a "little bit" of fried rice or an egg roll. Mother kept saying, "No I am not hungry right now." Then my sister mentioned, "Do not force mom to eat, but help her to be as comfortable as possible."

With mom not eating I think it disappointed Eugenia a bit, in the Filipino culture eating is a special way of bonding together at the moment. But Eugenia accepted Carol's comment and made sure everyone else ate well.

Mother kept munching on fresh red raspberries while resting and talking with each other, that was all she wanted to eat.

After lunch Alexis and Eugenia helped mother walk slowly back into her bedroom to rest, she was very tired. Alexis stayed in the bedroom with her grandmother. In a few minutes she returned from the bedroom wiping the tears from her eyes.

Then Eugenia wheeled me into mom's bedroom to visit with her. Setting near mom's bed, the three of us had a nice conversation for several minutes but I do not remember much that was said other than "I love you very much mom."

Mother and Eugenia added the same feelings, as Eugenia continued to make mom as comfortable as possible in bed,

"We will be back next Saturday to visit you again," Eugenia added, while pushing me out of mother's bedroom toward the living room where everyone was setting in silence.

The following Saturday morning Carol called and said mother had just passed away. Mother wanted to be cremated and have her ashes spread on our farm back home.

A few weeks later, Eugenia, Alexis and I flew to Indiana for mother's wake at the local Methodist Church. The church was almost within sight of where mother lived while growing up.

Mother's wake was filled with standing room only people, with her family, friends, neighbors and her fellow classmates were talking, laughing and hugging, which I enjoyed silently observing. It was nice to see the smiles and not the tears of sadness in mom's guests. The church prepared lunch to nearly three hundred people and they ran out of food.

Many people greeted me that I never met before. People said such things as,

"You do not know me but I went to school with your mother." There were people there that I never expected to see, some were my high school friends.

It took some maneuvering to get through the huge crowd of visitors to set in the back of the church basement was the best spot for me in my wheelchair. Once there I would be out of the way and people would not be tripping over my feet and I could see almost everyone.

Aunt Betty and I silently shared a smile and a hand wave to each other from half way across the church basement. She was suffering with Parkinson Disease and again I wish I could have gotten up and rightfully, respectfully, lovingly greeted my Aunt Betty Jean.

Every seat in the church basement was taken so many people were eating standing up.

Pictures were taken with a few classmates and others. Everyone was asking me about my daughter Alexis and they wanted to meet her. Alexis was there somewhere, but at the moment I did not see her, so I could not introduce my daughter to everyone.

A powerful emotional moment happened when one of my high school teachers greeted me in the back of the room, in high school he was our speech teacher but now he is a Reverend.

At mother's memorial, I was delighted to see him and greet each other as leaned forward to greet me. He said some mighty nice things to me as our foreheads touched and we looked at each other eyeball to eyeball, I had to cover my mouth to keep from crying is all I can remember. It was the respect that we had for each other, and the love of God, I am sure.

A Few of My Fears

A few of my fears is being financially broke, being burned by fire, house fires, drowning and being unable to move and in total helplessness. But I do not think I am afraid of death.

With my C. P. getting out of bed was never a major problem, when I used my crutches for leverage and support. My upper body strength was sufficient in rolling over in bed without assistance.

But after my spinal cord injury my body was almost useless in body movements. It is impossible to do the simplest things while lying in bed. With a great deal of work, while straining, sweating and wiggling my legs and arms I might be able to rollover myself, if I was not restricted with the blankets. Setting up in bed by myself is impossible without assistance.

A medical alert system is something that I could have used several times for security and safety. Three times was when I was riding in my electric wheelchair I lost my upper body balance and I fell over on my left side, unable to reach the joystick with my right hand.

Nearly four hours, all alone, I lost my balance, I was leaning over in my wheelchair, twisting my spine, and my ribs jammed on my wheelchair arm rest.

My body was so badly off balance, I could turn my head to the right and look at the ceiling but I did not have the strength or leverage to pull my body into a setting position. Then I was scared and angry at myself for being in my situation.

My left side of my body was the weakest side even with my Cerebral Palsy and with no balancing ability. But I always thought the spinal cord injury just made things ten times worse, more difficult or impossible to do.

Although, I had no fear of falling out of the wheelchair because the seat belt fit tightly around my lower abdomen to keep me safe from slipping out of the seat. My hips shifted off center nearly to the right side of the seat. The pain in my neck, back, ribs and hips was excruciating.

Panic overwhelmed me after my third frantic attempt to reach the power button before the control box goes into "sleep mode" and the joy stick would not function. Then I began to pray, "Oh Lord, please help me find a way to move my wheelchair so I can set myself up straight in my wheelchair." How I wished I had an emergency response button at that time.

My tee shirt was now drenched from sweat from straining to find a way to pull my body upright. The thin wet tee shirt rubbed against the vinyl seat back of the wheelchair irritating my skin. The gray padded vinyl arm rest was jammed tightly up under my left arm pit just added to my pain.

Now the irritation on my ribs, upper inside arm and arm pit was raw with the thrashing, straining and the jerking motions trying to toss my body upright so my right arm could relax and reach the right arm rest for leverage to pull myself upright.

There was no leverage from my feet or lower legs because my legs were stiff and straining searching for the wheelchair platform for my feet to hopefully push myself upright.

If only I had enough arm, hand and finger control I might have been able to push the release button on my seat belt. And free myself to slide out of the seat onto the den floor, maybe there I might be comfortable on the floor.

If only, if only, oh I hated this situation and myself. This was stupid on my part, for not having a back-up plan. After all, I never thought of falling over sideways in the wheelchair.

Time was measure by how many television shows passed. Finally after being in that awful, painful position Eugenia and Alexis came home and they rescued me and set me up right into a seating position.

Eugenia had several "why and how" questions to ask me but there was no answer to all of her questions except one, I just lost my balance and fell over.

Something had to change and get done so I would not hurt myself again, we needed a back-up plan to keep me from falling over sideways in my wheelchair. A gait belt buckled around by chest and wheelchair works quite well for my safety. But this just adds to my bondage issue on my helpless body.

A Partial List of Accomplishments

A few things that I have done:
Saved by Jesus

Swam (dog paddled wearing a ski belt) over and back across Cedar Lake in Howe, Indiana taking swimming lessons. This swim took me several hours with my swimming instructor by my side. Maybe a distance of two miles, I am not sure.

Worked in factories on the assembly line and offices

Learned to drive a car with hand brakes

Ordered and bought a brand new car and paid cash for it 1976 Chevy Nova with many optional features.

Graduated from a junior college, four year college and Graduate School and earned a few national academic honors

Traveled by airplane by myself to numerous cities in the United States.

Went on week long vacations by myself.

Married one time. I will soon be married thirty-six years

I am a dad and grandpa

Waded with my crutches into the Pacific and Atlantic Oceans.

Flew internationally to the Philippines via Canada, Okinawa, South Korea

Shot a rifle, BB guns and bow and arrows

I had a few car accidents but never a driving ticket.

Lived alone for a year in a different state and never knew anyone prior to moving.

Survived three surgeries on both ankles, both knees, both thighs and two surgeries on my neck.

For about three months I was in a body cast from my chest to my toes on both legs in the fourth grade.

I been on Highway 1 in California, visited the Grand Canyon, Yellowstone, Yosemite, Gulf Coast, Badlands, east coast, west coast, from California, Rhode Island, North Carolina and Florida

My longest drive by myself was from Knoxville, Tennessee to Wilmington, North Carolina

I came close to dying at least four or more times.

I been on local, national and international variety television shows and sporting events.

A former Miss North Carolina has been in our house and we are friends.

I was allowed to steer a small local airplane in flight with my hands.

I gave speeches in an auditorium in front of a few hundred people.

I was one of three students to represent our school in the 7th grade, in the county spelling contest.

I earned "Who's Who in American Junior Colleges 1974", (who and where is that doctor who said, I was not smart?)

I am a member of Phi Sigma Tau National Honor Society in Philosophy

Eugenia and I bought a house with a thirty year mortgage with no help and paid the loan off in seventeen years.

Drove a garden tractor to school because I could not walk to school.

Shook hands with a few major league baseball players.

Wrote a book and had it published.

Oh what am I forgetting……

Living In My Apartment

Living in northeastern Indiana and southern Michigan until I was thirty-two was very difficult during the winters. Walking with crutches and leg braces on the snow and ice was very dangerous.

For many years, my dream was to live somewhere it did not snow. But I wanted to live as close as possible to home in La Grange, Indiana. While attending college, I had a good friend in North Carolina. So I decided to move to North Carolina.

Dad offered to tow my car behind his van to Knoxville, Tennessee. At 3:30 a.m. December 1st, 1982 leaving home in an ice storm, together we took off in his van. He was headed to Florida for the winter and I continued on to North Carolina.

In Knoxville, dad took his van towing my car to a service station to reconnect the drive shaft in my car.

From Knoxville, Tennessee to Asheville, North Carolina was my longest drive in one day.

In Charlotte, I visited my college friend from Michigan, on my first day in North Carolina. Knowing one person in the state did give me some comfort. But still thinking Charlotte was too big for me.

From Charlotte to a stop in Fayetteville, to Wilmington, North Carolina I drove looking for a handicapped apartment. Trying on decide to which city would be best for me. Charlotte was quickly eliminated because of its size.

Wilmington was eliminated quickly because I could not find a handicapped apartment on a short notice and in a safe location. The possibility of hurricanes on the east coast scared me. Plus, I did not feel safe in driving in major city traffic with my cerebral palsy.

Living alone was extremely difficult. The weekly laundry was one of my hardest tasks while using my crutches. In college, the laundry room was just down the hall from my room. From there I could drag my heavy laundry bag back and forth to my room and laundry room.

From the city I decided to live in, I dragged the army bag full of laundry on the ground, like I pulled the wagon when feeding the pigs, from my apartment with my crutches, to the car, to the laundry mat, then back into my apartment. Doing the laundry always took several long exhausting hours on my crutches and it was a pain full task too.

Purchasing groceries was another difficult task that took all afternoon. At the grocery store, I pushed and guided the cart with my right hand down the aisles. The right crutch set in the grocery cart, while using one crutch on my left side to walk with and keep my balance.

Reaching for groceries from the higher or lower shelves was impossible or dangerous. If I leaned over to far reaching for groceries I could lose my balance and fall down. To avoid this embarrassment and humiliation I only purchased groceries that was within reach.

"Please do not put many things in one bag because the bag would be too heavy for me to carry with my crutches," I informed the cashier. Then the bag person would set the groceries in the trunk of my car. This was easier grabbing the groceries from the trunk and drag them to the kitchen table all by myself.

With the grocery bag handles looped around my right wrist on my crutches, I slowly and painfully took one bag at a time, partly full of groceries into my apartment. A long, tiring, painful task for just a few bags of groceries.

Sometimes at the grocery store a particular clerk would help me. She walked with me while pushing the grocery cart and gathering my groceries. Her helpfulness was so greatly appreciated and much easier and quicker for me.

Maybe others, will learn from my determination. Just doing, whatever that needs to be done, doing whatever it takes. We cannot give in or give up just when things get tiring or difficult. We just need to suck it up and work harder, find better ways and somehow continue on.

Certainly, I did not want people to think I was helpless. But I tried hard to prove to myself and other people that I was not helpless. Bernie and I explored in my counseling sessions, "that it was okay to ask for help and do not be afraid to ask." But that has never been easy for me to ask people for help.

The year that I lived alone, before my marriage to Eugenia, I tried very hard to keep my apartment clean, so I never baked in the oven, or cooked much of anything on the stove.

A friend from church offered to clean my apartment before Eugenia arrived from the Philippines. This was embarrassing to me, for her to do all of these things. She took my bedding and other laundry items to her house to wash and dry. She returned later and quickly put the sheets on the bed and put everything in their appropriate places.

My church friend certainly made a big improvement with the apartment's appearance. And I was very grateful and thankful for her helpfulness and kindness.

Over the decades, I became a bit bitter over things with churches, agencies, organizations, neighbors, general people and friends. The great people of the United States, helps people in disasters locally and all over the world, that is wonderful and we should.

Everyone who knows or sees me could tell that I was disabled, but rarely did anyone offer assistance. If they had offered assistance, chances are I might have turned down their kind offers, depending on the circumstances, but those people are never forgotten.

There are things called, pride, dignity and class, a thin line away from waiting for or expecting help and helplessness. Even though, I learned through personal counseling, "it is okay to ask for help, no matter what the reason is." It is tough measuring up with the non-challenged people, when everything I did or tried to do, was so very difficult or impossible.

But two things I think surprised my friend: One the electric cooking stove and oven was clean because I cooked with an electric skillet and a microwave oven. And two she commented with wonder, on the refrigerator.

"Lonnie?" she asked with astonishment, with one hand on the refrigerator door and her other hand on her hip. A little embarrassment swept over me knowing what she seen, "Why do you have canned food and nothing else in your refrigerator to eat?"

"Well," I stammered, "the refrigerator is the easiest place for me to store food," I tried reasoning my decision with her. Because I am unable to reach the overhead or lower cupboards and keep my balance on my crutches to store the food in the proper place.

There she stood, momentarily looking at my canned food in the refrigerator. She gave me no clue, idea or hint on what she may have been thinking at that moment. But finally, I believe she understood my reasoning.

When I lived alone I never ate at the dining table setting down, I ate leaning against the kitchen counter top because I was afraid of falling down with the food or dropping the food on the floor.

You can be assured I never missed our church dinners. The Pastor always told me, "Just show up. You do not need to bring any food."

It only took one invitation from another elderly church couple, for me to start showing up at their house and eating a few meals weekly with them. Their friendship and her great cook and eating there was a great blessing, which made my life at meal time much easier.

Eugenia immediately took over these difficult duties for me upon her arrival. She mentioned in her letters, she knew how to cook Filipino food but she was not familiar cooking American food. Eugenia is a wonderful cook with Filipino and American foods. Oh I am so blessed that Eugenia married me.

First Time I Seen Eugenia

"How can you love someone you never seen or kissed?" my college friend asked referring to the letter, that was on my desk.

"I just feel it in my heart," I replied excitedly, showing him a picture of my Filipina pen pal.

"That could be some other person," he teased me. For nearly two years I heard negative comments from friends about my pen pal relationship with Eugenia. Do not marry or bring her here. She will get here, take your money and run off, people kept saying.

A few months earlier, I read a magazine ad, "Correspond with Filipinas." What I have to lose, I reasoned. Quickly, I mailed the ad back the correspondence company.

After anxiously waiting for several long weeks there on the brown carpet, shoved under my dorm door was a large yellow enveloped.

Hurriedly, I flipped the heavy book satchel off my shoulder onto the bed. The yellow envelope was gently grabbed with the two crutch tips, as if I was picking something up with tweezers.

Then I flipped the yellow enveloped onto my bed with my crutches, The envelope was from the correspondence company.

My goal was to find a Filipina pen pal and nothing more at the time. Quickly I filled in the section on myself and who I wanted to correspond with. And she must speak English.

Honestly, I was interested in someone smart, strong willed and college educated. The twenty dollars application fee was a hefty amount. And the thought of being ripped off by the ad agency did cross my mind.

And anxiously, I looked forward in receiving my first letter. Over three months passed, and I received three letters from three Filipina. But nothing what the ad stated, I could receive hundreds of letters from Filipinas."

Rebecca from Cebu was the first Filipina to write me. She was studying to be a mid-wife. With her short black hair and wearing her white student nursing uniform and she looked like a little doll. Her dream was to help take care of her family.

The second Filipina, who wrote was Inday, a senior in college studying Civil Engineering.

My third letter arrived, a short time later under my dorm door. Hurriedly, I sat down and grabbed the letter with my crutches. The letter was from the Philippines and I ripped open the envelope. The hand written letter, was dated September 1, 1980. Two weeks later to reach me by airmail.

The letter began, "Friend," that was a nice appropriate greeting, I thought while continuing to quickly read. Quote, "Hi! A very pleasant day to you, at the very outset. Just let me call you friend. Maybe you're surprised upon receiving this letter of mine." Wow, I was thinking, surprised at this moment.

Quote, "To make my letter short I was able to know your name, address and telephone through channels. A friend of my friend gave me your name and address, I told her that I want to have a pen pal and preferably a foreigner. So she answers my dreams."

A couple years later Eugenia told me, she put the list of pen pal names in her drawer and forgot about the list. But she came upon the list again while cleaning out her dresser.

Out of random and me a college student Eugenia said, she chose my name from a list of names and wrote me a letter.

Jesus knew what He was doing all along. Many times this list could have been lost, or Eugenia could have chosen another name.

Eugenia first introduced herself as Eugenia, but her friends called her Eugene. And her profession was teaching. Eugene is a very beautiful woman, smart, hardworking and very caring. I thought to myself.

Her hobbies were crocheting, spinning records, taking care of animals, pets and gardening. And she loved cooking. That same evening I wrote Eugenia my first letter. This was exciting but scared too, I needed to tell her how happy I was and be honest and tell her, I was born physically handicapped, with Cerebral Palsy. And explain how I was affected with Cerebral Palsy. However, I did not want to scare her away either.

Eugenia's second letter arrived a few weeks later and she explained, "I accept you as you are. And no further explanation is needed." In fact, Eugenia continued, "please stop writing to me about your handicap or I will stop writing to you. Just get plenty of rest and sleep." Then I almost cried. My Cerebral Palsy was alright with her.

For nearly two years we exchanged letters and gifts. Now, I wanted to bring Eugenia to the states. But we needed someone who may be willing to sponsor Eugenia through Immigrations.

There were two people I wanted to share our plans, our relationship and sponsorship with. Both of these people attended Graduate School classes with me

Our plans were not well received by the Filipina doctor. She stated firmly, she believed Eugenia was taking advantage of me, a free ride, to get into the United States. And I should not bring Eugenia to the U.S. And the doctor continued, "She could divorce you or leave you after she gets her green card."

This was disappointing but I was not totally surprised. Her negativity made me more determined. Someone should be willing to help us and I needed to find that person. With the non-support from many people, I decided to keep quiet. Even to the point

"I was not writing to her anymore," if someone asked.

Eugenia also asked me to send her letters to a different address. Her Auntie did not approve of us corresponding, but we kept on secretly writing. One evening, I called another Graduate School classmate, a retired dentist to ask him about sponsoring Eugenia.

"Hello Bob here. May I help you," Bob answered.

"Hello this is Lonnie", I said in my nervous Cerebral Palsy effected voice, trying to forcing myself to breathe deeply to speak more clearly.

"Bob", I continued, "Do you know of anyone who may be interested in sponsoring my pen pal Eugenia, here from the Philippines?" I nervously asked. Bob had heard that I have been writing to a young woman from the Philippines. My fist grip relaxed a bit on the telephone receiver which I held firmly against my ear.

Bob was interested in my story, so he stopped by my dorm room two days later to discuss this further. Bob did visit and I briefly shared Eugenia's and my story and some pictures with him. He also suggested it would be easier for me if Eugenia visited here first because of my Cerebral Palsy. And he expressed his support with Eugenia's sponsorship.

"Bob thank you for your helpfulness. But why did you agree to help so quickly when everyone else refused?" I asked.

"Because I cannot destroy your dreams Lonnie," he added.

For the first time, in nearly two years I felt positive in bringing Eugenia to the United States.

Bob thought it could be a few short weeks before INS requested information on airplane tickets for Eugenia's transportation but nothing seriously happened.

Upon completing Graduate School and the Graduate Counseling Internship at a nursing home back home in Indiana, I was relocating to North Carolina by myself. This was not an easy with my Cerebral Palsy. But I have been planning of relocating for a decade.

Moving far away from home was scary. The physical difficulties of living alone, such as falling down and injuring myself would happen in time. But before I left Indiana, a big event happen to me.

"Lon, wake up its four a.m. Eugene is on the telephone. Hurry up, a collect call too," mom said while shaking me one morning.

"Eugene?" I quickly said waking up.

"Hello Eugene? I answered wide awake and excited.

"I love you. I love you. I love you," Eugenia said with her soft, excited voice. That was all she said at the beginning of our first live conversations over the telephone from the Philippines.

"I love you too," I hurriedly said while smiling and interrupting her.

She wanted to call and wish me a safe trip to North Carolina and get "plenty of rest," Our conversation was short, nice and special to and hear her voice after writing letters to each other for a year.

A Pastor and a church deacon named Joe came to visit me in my apartment on afternoon after arriving at my chosen destination in North Carolina.

The two major topics I shared with Pastor and Joe was how I left Indiana and arrived in here a day earlier.

My second topic was Eugenia our relationship, our dreams and complications with Immigrations in bringing Eugenia here to the United States.

"We will get her here. Jesus wants good things for the people who follow Him," Pastor added smiling.

Twice, the Pastor called the INS office, including the American Embassy in Manila, to check and ask on what documents were needed to speed the process up for Eugenia's Visa status.

Over the past few months, actually nothing was going on with INS. Eugenia was traveling hours by bus and waiting in line all day, for many days, by herself at the

American Embassy in Manila. Still nothing was being accomplished, another dead end for us.

We were frustrated and angry in dealing with INS from both countries. Over two and a half years we had unnecessary delays, pay offs with officials, fees, runarounds, out dated applications and general red tape hassles. But we were not going to give up.

Typing applications for INS was impossible with my stiff, painful fingers, I did not have a computer or electric typewriter for me to use during this time either and the INS documents required type written.

The office manager of the apartment complex where I lived, volunteered to type all the documents that INS requested. She was a major impact with her quick work typing the documents, in communicating and submitting forms to the INS. The whole process was just a long run with delays and inconveniences in both counties with the INS.

If needed, I was willing to travel to the Philippines but that would be very difficult for me. Eugenia earlier expressed to just wait for her in North Carolina.

After visiting a local travel agency, I learned that there were only two airlines that had daily flights from Manila to the United States.

That evening I wrote letters to both airlines CEO's with detailed information on the dreams that Eugenia and I have on meeting each other. Enclosed in both letters was a newspaper article featuring my story about my handicap and the long distance relationship with Eugenia.

And I asked if they would consider giving Eugenia a free flight over here. In my letters, I informed them how Eugenia and I met, how the relationship developed over the years and I was a student putting myself through college and about my condition with Cerebral Palsy.

One airlines President replied, "We receive many requests from families on transportation and our policy was to deny all requests," unquote. This was just another option that did not work out the way I hoped it would. There must be another option to bring us together that I have not explored yet.

Daily I prayed that new avenues would open, we certainly needed help and good news with Eugenia and her flight.

Sometime later, the Chairman of the Board from another major international airlines replied, "...we receive many requests..." oh no I thought not again. "...on complimentary transportation from many people and because of the amount of requests they are all denied"...I thought again another form letter, a rejection..."However, we decided to give Miss ------ complimentary transportation because we feel you have a most interesting story..." Her maiden name was removed in my writings.

Suddenly, I began shaking. Laying the letter on my desk, so I would not drop it. My voice yelled loudly with excitement, "Praise God. Yes," while pounding my brown, cluttered desk, with my right hand.

It is just by coincidence that Pan Am, has opened up a new hub in Raleigh, North Carolina. And we would be happy to give Miss (name withheld by me) complimentary tickets from Manila to Raleigh.

Everything will be arrangement along with a tour of New York City. We will contact you further on information concerning Miss (name withheld by me) flight information.

Sincerely,
Mr. (name withheld by me)
Chairman of the Board, (airlines name with held by me.) Unquote.

Another Jesus miracle in this development from the airlines CEO. Our dreams were beginning to fall into place with the blessings from Jesus and from the helpfulness of other people.

However, there was no progress on Eugenia's Visa from INS over the past year, total gridlock. So I sent a letter to my U. S. Senator, asking if he would look into our situation with INS.

Within a week, my Senator answered and stated he had contacted INS in and asked for top priority in Eugenia's case. Soon after the Senator's letter, I received a letter from INS requesting specific documents for Eugenia's passport approval.

While setting in the Pastor's office, I listened to his conversation with the American Embassy in Manila, Philippines. We learned the hold up with the passport approval was an official document to show proof of financial responsibility for Eugenia that could have been requested two tears earlier.

Over six months earlier I submitted a document showing my income. But the lady explained they needed a similar document that needed notarization.

"Why didn't they tell me this last year?" I asked in frustration anger.

Months earlier I mentioned to Eugenia in my letters, to pack everything she wants to bring to the States on a short notice. This financial responsibility documented for Eugenia needed to be at the American Embassy in Manila with in twenty-four hours before Eugenia's Visa deadline expired.

Until then, we never knew the Visa had been issued to her. Later this deadline was waived, most likely through my Senator's office.

Upon sharing this situation with Donna she immediately walked through an adjoining door to share with Kathy, the secretary of an attorney's office.

Kathy called many, overnight delivery businesses searching for the best service and prices. Finally she had a price, a pick up time and a guarantee delivery time, overnight to the American Embassy in Manila for our document.

A whopping ninety-five dollars. "Whatever it takes to get the document there," I said rushing off to the bank for the money order. The discussions between all of us that morning was, "this document better get first class seats and attention on the airplane."

"Lonnie," Joe excitedly greeting me, while I climbed his cement steps at his house, "Eugenia called here a few hours ago collect and I refused her call," he stammered out disappointed in his reply to Eugenia, knowing that Eugenia and I did not have a telephone.

"Oh no, Joe," I surprisingly said since Joe knew Eugenia did not have a private telephone.

Joe continued speaking and apologizing, "Eugenia called you were not here and I was not thinking and I am so very sorry for refusing Eugenia's collect call."

"That is OK Joe. There is nothing we can do about it now." My thoughts were wondering why was Eugenia calling?

"If Eugenia calls here again, please be sure to take her collect call for me," I said.

"I can assure you. Next time Eugenia calls. I will gladly accept her call and not make that blunder again," Joe said, disappointed in his actions. Especially, since Joe offered to accept collect telephone calls from Eugenia.

Joe's cancer was in remission and he wanted so much to be helpful in his own way. Eugenia told me later, when her collect call was refused she sat down on the sidewalk next to the phone booth on the street cried and cried.

The next evening Eugenia did return her collect call, this time Joe accepted Eugenia's call.

"Where have you been all day", my Pastor asked while approaching me in the church parking lot.

"No place special why?" I asked, wondering why I was so important to find me on a Monday afternoon.

"The American Embassy called and said Eugene's visa was approved. She is scheduled to leave Manila Wednesday, Thursday our time," Pastor said smiling and excited for us.

During those three days Eugenia packed her luggage and said good-bye to her family and friends. Eugenia did not have time to say good-bye to everyone before leaving the Philippines.

Tears came to my eyes. For an instant I was unable to relax to talk clearly with my Pastor. We were both very happy, beaming with big smiles on our faces in learning this great news.

"Thank you Jesus," we prayed to Jesus giving thanks to Him and prayed for a safe trip to Eugenia. That night, I did not sleep from this excitement.

A young church couple opened their house for Eugenia to live with them until our wedding. INS allowed us ninety days to get married so our wedding date was within the time allowed by eleven days.

On the eve of Eugenia's arrival in Raleigh, North Carolina I called her at the Howard Johnson Hotel near the John F Kennedy International Airport in New Your City to welcome her to the United States and wish her Happy Birthday. She sounded excited but tired.

This third time that we spoke to each other on the telephone in nearly two and one half years of writing each other. The helpful airlines gave Eugenia her a first class seat ticket from Manila to JFK airport. And the seat next to Eugenia's was unused, so Eugenia had enough room on her flight to rest.

The airlines assigned a Filipina representative to greet Eugenia as she exited the aircraft and help

Eugenia with the luggage and escorted Eugenia to the hotel for overnight until Eugenia's connecting flight to Raleigh the next afternoon. And the airlines paid for Eugenia's hotel room and offered Eugenia a tour of New Your City.

To surprise Eugenia with flowers on our first meeting face to face, in my excitement, I purchased a dozen long stem red roses in a tall green glass vase.

"Lonnie, it might be a good idea if we take the flowers back to the house with this glass vase," my friend said as she climbed up into the van upon leaving the florist.

Reminding myself to keep calm, not be in a hurry and not fall down was not helpful, still excited and nervous waiting for Eugenia. The long walk through the airport terminal on my crutches was tiring

Time went by slowly before passengers began emerging from the gate. Many passengers came through the gate quickly but Eugenia from the pictures she sent me, was not among them.

"What is keeping her?" I asked she must be the last person off the airplane.

"There she is." I smiled broadly, recognizing Eugenia. She wore her long black shiny hair pulled back off her face, carrying several bags and her purse.

"Eugene, I love you," was my first words ever spoken to her face to face. "Welcome to the United States. It is so, good to see you." I whispered softly smiling at

Eugenia. We hugged warmly and looked at each other closely. Eugenia was even more beautiful than I had imagined and shorter than I was.

"Walk slowly," Eugenia said, while we walked arm in arm through the airport to the elevator, while my friends carried Eugenia's luggage.

It was impossible for me jostling on my crutches to hold Eugenia's hand or put my arm around Eugenia, a big deal for me but this is the way it is for me.

We were quiet several moments at the terminal, it was a joy to take in all of our emotions and be together for the very first time. We kept looking at each other, realizing that Jesus had finally brought us together after all this time.

On the way home, we held hands, then Eugenia slipped a ring on my little finger, the only finger the ring fit. The street lights were on and the gold ring, brightly shined between our fingers while holding hands. In the Philippines she had the ring engraved, "Lonnie / Eugene 9-21-80." The date she received my first letter.

Eugenia mentioned INS notified her to pick up her Visa at the Philippine Embassy and informed her in three days she would be leaving. During these three days Eugenia packed her luggage said good-bye to her family and friends.

September 21st is a significant date in our lives forever.

September 21st, 1980 Eugenia received my fist letter.

September 21st, 1983 Eugenia left the Philippines crossing the International Dateline.

September 21st, 1983 Eugenia arrived in the United States.

September 21st, is Eugenia's birthday.

September 21st, is Eugenia's older brother "Kuya" birthday.

On our first evening together our friends were excited talking with Eugenia and showing Eugenia where her bedroom would be until our wedding day. And all three of them including Eugenia were busy bringing in Eugenia's luggage.

Excited and a little nervous I sat on the living room couch watching the joy of welcoming Eugenia into her now temporary home. Wishing I could be of some help. But I was happy Eugenia was finally here with me, I love her so very much.

"Eugene," our friend called. Eugenia emerging from the bedroom, "Yes Ma'am," replied Eugenia.

"Please, call me by my name. But how do you pronounce your name"? She asked. "My real name is Eugenia but you can call me Eugene. And Eugenia is pronounced as (U- hain- ya)," in the Philippines", added Eugenia smiling.

The next day I introduced Eugenia to our Pastor. He was a tremendous help, for me from the first moment I met him, the first week of January 1983.

On December 10th 1983 Eugenia and I were married. Joe had the honor of escorting Eugenia up the aisle.

Attitude

Quote, "As a child, Lon, even with tears on your face, you were stronger than most of us can ever strive to be. Blessings to you." Unquote by Sharon.

Sharon and her family, all played a significant part of my life in numerous ways.

Our attitude is a way of thinking that affects a person's behavior. Nobody has a great attitude every day. Happening in everyone's life affects one's attitude.

Circumstance affects my attitude when I want things done and I cannot do things by myself such as cleaning up a cluttered area or picking up something that I dropped on the floor.

This is always frustrating to me when I cannot continue on with my immediate plans. The frustrations are then followed by anger and self- hate or worthlessness because I could not do what I wanted to.

Sometimes in asking for things brought back the feelings "can't never did anything," or "what good are you," so I would try and try different ways to accomplish something or just forget about the original project or plans all together.

At some point we decide we did our best and not worry about the small things is often difficult for me. Maybe I would have succeeded in some tasks if I had done things differently. But I cannot go through life thinking that way. This reasoning is something that I must get better at.

When I am frustrated I must stop and think about all of the blessings that Jesus has given me. Think about all of the positive things that I have accomplished. Then continue on and build my positive attitude on these beliefs. All of these thoughts are needed to feel good about myself.

When "I learned it was okay and to not feel guilty in asking for help," during my personal counseling sessions and I began feeling better about myself.

Long ago our good friends gave me a birthday gift a tee shirt. On the printed shirt was a man resting in a reclining chair, holding his television remote control. The quote on the shirt was, "I'd help you, but I am stuck to this chair." Unquote.

That shirt and quote expressed precisely what was truly in my heart, I feel like I am "stuck." Trapped in bondage, in this wheelchair and body, wanting and waiting to do everything that I possibly could with a normal body, to get up help myself and others.

Some military people have said things like, "I have spent years fighting in the Vietnam War," and I respect that. But my thinking is, "I have spent my whole life fighting battles or wars between my mind and body with this physical disability and psychological pain."

How Can I Help You?

"How are you doing? What's going on? "are questions people ask me, it depends upon my attitude and physical pain at any moment. Those are fair questions but no fault or disrespect for people but at times I immediately become offended. Every day, I try to do my best for myself and others.

There is no joy being physically dependent on others and interrupt their plans. The freedom of independents from other people is one of God's gifts of life.

It is upsetting to not be able to do something that I need or want done, these issues develop into the helplessness and worthless feelings. Especially, when I cannot get things done while being strapped in a body that does not work, setting in a electrical wheelchair.

Instead of hearing, "How are you doing?" or "what is going on?' I would much rather hear "What do you need?", "How can I help?" "What would you like to talk about?" or maybe just say something nice and positive and let the conversation continue naturally. These questions are action positive questions which would help me become more comfortable in my physical circumstance.

And I must learn to feel comfortable with myself and the things that I cannot do after I broke my neck. Such as the life activities that I could do by myself with Cerebral Palsy even with my difficulty, things such as cutting up my food to eat, drinking from a glass in my hand, getting in and out of bed myself or rolling over in bed.

Including the physical transfers in and out of automobiles, transfers on the toilet, showers, buttons, zippers, buckles, my hand writing. But with my spinal cord injury, almost everything in the normal daily activity became impossible for me to do.

We must stop thinking about ourselves and our short comings and think on how we can positive influence our lives and society. Countless people are watching my personal actions on how I go about living. And I must do good things so others might learn to do good things in their life circumstances.

One afternoon, I was having lunch with the General Manager of a Major League Baseball Team, when he asked me if I needed help in cutting my meat.

His offer was thankfully declined because I needed to show my friend, who I have met through correspondence, that I could cut the meat myself. Being handicapped does not mean I am helpless and I do not need help in every situation. But I am sure Joe's offer to help cut my meat was with kindness.

More importantly, I was trying very hard to make a great, lasting impression on Mr. Brown. My purpose in meeting with him was to pursue my dream, to be a Major League Baseball Administrator.

For nearly six years, I had free box seat tickets to the major league baseball games and we had meetings in his office, discussing my goals.

These meetings with my great friend, gave me motivation and inspiration to this day, because he never asked, "What is going on?" but rather he showed me interest and asked questions such as "How can I help you? This is what you need to do." But most of all Joe added encouragement, support and helpfulness to help keep my dreams and goals alive.

If you are speaking with someone who could use a little help, do not start with such questions as, "What is going on?" but rather, "If you need anything, let me know."

Medical Appointments

Medical appointments, the difficulty and waiting is not fun. We must be innovative to position the wheelchair as close as possible to the dental chairs or examination tables for transfer safely but there is rarely enough adequate space.

It is difficult to move my body without pain even with assistance, which is always Eugenia, doing all the heavy lifting of my body.

Dental chairs can be raised or lowered. Medical examination tables are stationary and are much too high to get up onto.

In most cases, the arm rests on the dental chairs are not removable. Or move in the wrong direction for safe transfers from my wheelchair.

In my opinion, the less ambulatory and the elderly may not be able to get the medical procedures they need, because of lack of wheelchair maneuverability space and transferring limitations.

One time a doctor ordered me an ultra sound exam. The examination table was higher than my waist. Immediately, this was a major problem for me to get on the examination table, I could not just "hop" up on the medical examination table, I needed to be lifted up onto the table.

From years of previous transfer experiences, I always wore a patient transfer belt around my waist for safety reasons. Eugenia's health and safety was always at risk too.

Preceding one examination, I told the nurse I needed assistance to safely and easily transfer me up onto the CT examination table. The technician quickly left and returned with a male assistant.

Now I was feeling a little more comfortable with my transfer "up onto" the medical table with a big muscular man there to help assist in my transfer.

Eugenia positioned herself into her normal transfer position in front of me and unfastened my wheelchair seat belt to transfer me up onto the examination table. Mind you Eugenia is about three inches shorter and thirty pounds lighter than me.

Discreetly Eugenia unfastened the transfer belt over my lap towel to keep the towel from falling to the floor and exposing my open fly and penis to the two helpers.

Everyone was set in position with my right arm around Eugenia's neck as she gripped my transfer belt with one hand on each side of my waist. This transfer technique is very similar to firmly hugging each other.

Then we began a rocking motion to gather momentum for this transfer. And I was trying to tighten my leg muscles with hope to have some rigid support in my legs in transferring.

The CT technician was immediately to my left, with her hands on my back and the big man stood observing everything. All set, Eugenia pulled me out of the wheelchair but the women could not get my bottom up onto the examination table which was higher than my waist.

The pain shot from my lower back from arthritis and my legs went weak. Instinctively, Eugenia tried setting me back in the wheelchair but my bottom missed the wheelchair and I went nearly down to the floor.

My knees was wrenching in hot pain because my tendons behind my knees since my knee surgery could not bend much more than in a seating position.

"My knee, my knee," I yelled in pain. The lady technician grabbed my bottom to help get me back up and somehow the two women managed to get me up onto the CT table.

Still in extreme pain in my tendons in my knees, shoulders and my lower back I opened my eyes after a second and noticed the man standing down by the foot of the examination table.

If anything, all the guy did was grab my legs to maybe keep me from rolling off the other side of the table.

We starred at each other in silence, as I was wrenching and moaning in excruciating pain in my lower back and especially in my knees, because they were bent to far from my fourth grade knees surgery would allow. But I gave him the meanest look that I ever gave to anyone. The guy did nothing in helping me transfer. Within a flash, he left the room.

After my examination the two women guided me back into the wheelchair without a major problem. Realizing while I laid on that table in pain, Jesus gave me another national or international project to work on.

This project will require all medical and dental offices, to have a manual patient hoist with supporting equipment for all patients that needs transfer assistance with trained technicians.

Medical buildings and offices costing millions of dollars, surely a medical establishment could afford a couple thousand dollars for a medical transfer hoist.

Several dozens of "Letters to the Editor" have been submitted to numerous newspapers so far, across the United States concerning this problem.

Many, elderly and disabled people are pushed down the list of priorities on accommodations in the medical examination rooms and procedures. Some disabled people might not have their examinations because it is so difficult and painful to deal with.

But one big issue with the doctor's offices, medical offices, hospitals and clinics will be the liability, physical issues with the insurance companies. And who other than me perhaps to change the laws and procedures for safe transfers for the elderly, disabled and the medical profession.

Until That Time Comes

Until I leave for Heaven, I must keep working to be the best person that I can be. However imperfect, I must keep working, fighting, and teaching others, especially to my daughter Alexis and my grandsons, Ashton and Ace to the best of my ability, they should never give up on their hopes and dreams.

As I get older, it is more important on what can I do for others. What can I do to teach others to be more comfortable around disabled people, including how disabled people can be comfortable with themselves.

This is the constant battle and task that I must work on to control each day of my life. The battle of, wanting to do something for others, versus the battle of not being able to do something.

We must find that inner peace within ourselves to say it is alright, if you can no longer be able to do what you wish to do. However, accepting limitations is not declaring defeat.

One day I asked my friend, to hang a poster on my bedroom wall which reads, "JESUS the Savior." Jesus has been my Savior since March 1972 and we should cast all of our troubles and concerns onto him. At times for me, this is easier said than done. This poster also helps me find my peace. Jesus knows what we are going through.

People are watching every move I make and judging me, as is Jesus. My joys is going shopping with Eugenia and observing people. These people's decisions are based upon my actions, perhaps influencing their thoughts on disabled people, so I must do my best in everything.

When we look people in the eye and smile, sometimes we might get a smile in return. With our looks and interactions with others, we show a snapshot of our character to the world.

Picking Things Up

"Lonnie, did you say you use pencils to type and what do you use to hold down two keys at once can you use both of your hands?" my Internet friend asked.

Her question was appreciated, I type with a broken plastic window blind rod in my right hand. My left thumb is solely used for the left shift key, I cannot use any fingers to type with.

There are three plastic broken window blind rods on my desk that I type with, one key stroke I peck away at a time, I need extra typing rods in case I drop them from my numb, tingling hands and I drop many things often.

On one "pointer stick "I asked my daughter to slip a binding paper clip on one end. When I drop the pointer stick, I get the broom stick that has a magnet taped on one end to retrieve my pointer stick.

On my desk there is a wooden dole, similar to a broom stick about thirty inches long. One end of the dole we drilled a hole to thread a long shoe string through the dole and we tied the shoe string onto the "desk stick."

When I drop the desk stick, I get another broom stick and hook the broom stick through the shoe string on the desk stick, then I can pick up the desk stick up off the floor.

The desk stick, I use for many things, exercising, dialing on the touch button desk phone, reaching for objects on furniture, light switches, thermostat, TV remote control, etc.

Another problem is retrieving dropped computer mouse ball. This is difficult strapped in a wheelchair when the reacher's are too short to reach the objects I want.

But I found a small plastic bag that had loops for handles and I grabbed a broom stick handle. Setting in my wheelchair with the white plastic bag and the wooden broom handle in my hand, I dropped the plastic bag on the floor near the computer mouse ball.

Softly I tap the computer mouse ball into the plastic bag, like playing golf. Now I was excited and exhausted with this small progress. The grooves on the end of the of the broom stick, easily kept the plastic bag from slipping off the broom stick.

After I lifting the bag about head high, I eased my hands down the broom handle and grabbed the bag and put the computer mouse ball back into the computer mouse, this took nearly an hour to accomplish but I did it.

Velcro would work nicely for securing TV remote control on my desk, but another expense. These are a few examples of improvising ideas that I use in my daily living.

Difficulty Shaving

One summer morning around 2012, I felt my body was not functioning well. This seemed silly, after a life time with Cerebral Palsy and over a decade with a spinal cord fracture. So I mentioned my concerns, maybe I had a mini-stroke to my doctor. Within a few days we learned that my brain scan was "negative."

So I asked, if my brain showed any injury causing my Cerebral Palsy at birth. Looking in the mirror at the left side of my skull looked "dented," in my view from using forceps. He said no, but my cerebral palsy might have occurred in another artery.

All my life I was told that I had brain damaged. My confusion just raised more questions, "Why didn't the damage brain appear on my CT Scan?" Maybe the forceps did damage my brain. But perhaps the real issue was during my birthing process when my brain was not receiving the blood supply or oxygen, I will never know.

It took a good while and great effort to sort of play tricks between my mind and body to get my body to cooperate with my mind. And often that trick was to get my mind away from the struggle of my body.

One of these tricks I learned at the children's hospital when the doctor was trying to bend my knees. Suddenly the doctor starting saying various types of food to trick my mind into breaking the spastic tension in my legs and knees to bend more freely. At the same time, the doctor applied gentle pressure on my legs to get them to bend more freely.

But wiggling and tricking my body into this particular position of setting on the edge of my bed and twisting on the hip so I could bend my knees to put my shoes on was not easy and painful.

Other things I was unable to do with my arms and hands I could never turn my hands palms up. And I held a spoon or fork with my palms down. While getting dressed I insert the belt through the belt loops in the slacks, before putting on my slacks. And I used the crutches to start all of the clothing over my feet. It amazed me how dad could get dressed in a matter of a few seconds.

Subconsciously, I could never "measure up" to be to be the person physically that I wanted to be, like my dad, Doug and many others. But notice what I have accomplished, in other ways considering my difficult hurdles.

It is difficult to accept my helplessness and still believe "I was still okay, no matter what." Psychologically, maybe not much is a big deal, until you lose the ability to do what you want to do.

Prior to the mid nineteen-seventies I could do a normal handshake. T hen the pain and tightness began in my right arm. Those fancy handshakes that athlete's do I marveled and wished that I could do them too.

This is when I began going to several different types of doctors and therapies almost ten years. Yet nothing helped my body to get to the point where it was fairly easy or comfortable in just moving about.

My body was not part of who I wanted to be. In my mind, I could choose to be ambulatory, but my body would not cooperate with my thoughts. My body betrayed me somehow and I was angry at myself and God. The pain, the restriction never left my body and medications did not help. Feeling discouraged I quit visiting doctors for my neck and arm problems.

When I fell and broke my neck in the bathroom, I lost most of my body's ability to function as before.

My shaving is done with my right hand while turning my head to the right and guiding the razor with both hands on my left cheek because of my weaker left side.

My fingers were numb and felt stiff and four times larger than what they actually were. My body looks quite normal, until I actually physically moved. My physical movements reminded me it was in slow motion with no smooth fluid motion.

After my spinal cord injury, I was not able to urinate in a toilet, I needed to use a plastic hand held urinal. So accidents often happens in wetting my pants with my stiff, numb fingers. And I could not manipulate buttons and zippers on my clothes. Our improvised idea that worked best by covering myself by using a hand towel.

The muscle spasms, Charlie horses and saddle sores, consumed my body on almost a daily and nightly basis and also raising havoc creating psychologically stress.

As a premature baby I rarely cried and later on in life I could not run to expand my lungs. As an adult I have major problems breathing correctly, I am unable to blow up a balloon or yell or talk very loud.

Learning to breathe deeply, which often I am unable to do, my doctor suggested blowing bubbles through a straw into big jug of soapy water.

Years ago, a stranger sent me an instant message concerning his grade school daughter who had cerebral palsy. In his message, he asked for advice on how to improve his daughter's handwriting.

Understandably, I knew what he and his daughter was going through with her struggles. It was a blessing to share how my hand writing improved when I wrote on a flat student desk top.

And I continued on, he might try to child's wrist weight to help control his daughter's muscle spasms. The father never contacted me again but I do hope his daughter had some success with my advice.

Nothing for me is ever easy. When life seems unfair and not worth continuing, somehow we must search very deeply into our souls and our faith to continue on living.

My College Friend on Facebook

One day I posted on Facebook, "Eternal life, no pain, no wheelchairs, in Heaven thank God, I'm ready."

My college friend, who I have not seen or heard from, for a few decades made the comment below on my Facebook post.

My friend said and I quote, "I totally understand feeling that way. When you live with chronic pain and limits of physical mobility, the idea of being completely free of that is very enticing.

When we feel overwhelmed, it's easy to start thinking about how much easier it would be to just let go and sink into negative thoughts and start to lose motivation for living well - as well as we can, with all of our limitations and challenges.

But along with the limitations, challenges and pain, there are good times and wonderful experiences and the people with whom we share those experiences. Great music, old movies you love, a beautiful sunset, watching the snow falling, your favorite food, laughing and swapping stories ... all with people you love to be with. Especially the ones who make you smile, just thinking about them. Like your daughter and your grandsons. And the wife who takes such good care of you.

Now, those are all the reasons why you will miss living all the life God wants you to live. What about all the people who would miss you? And miss your sense of humor, your writing and all the ideas that only you come up with, all the people who are given the chance to meet their personal challenges by helping you, being of service of you. We are, every one of us, either teacher or student to someone, at one time or another, in our lives.

You aren't done learning and you aren't done teaching. Try to make peace with the limitations, by focusing not on what you cannot do, but WHAT YOU STILL CAN DO.

The pain, however, is personal, very individual. Some people can find ways to cope with it mentally and physically, through medications or physical therapy or counseling and prayer.

Others have a more difficult time. Some days are better than others. So, just take it a day at a time. Take it an hour at a time, if necessary. Tell yourself you can wait it out for another hour. You can stand anything for a short time, right? When that hour is up, give yourself another hour.

Whatever it takes. Just get through whatever pain you have to endure and the dark thoughts that frequently go along with it, because there's a huge pile of reasons why you still need to be here and keep trying.

Whenever you lose sight of that, look at a picture of your grandson. Think of how many things you still have to teach him, tell him about.

It may seem inviting to think about getting to the next stage of existence sooner than God wants you to, but that's up to him. No, Lonnie you are not done yet." Unquote.

From my college friend.

Is Cerebral Palsy Hereditary

In 1973, I became concerned if my Cerebral Palsy could be heredity. So I sent a letter to my friend Ms. Anita an administrator at the Cerebral Palsy Clinic.

Within a few weeks she replied, from my best memory it read in part, I quote Ms. Anita, "…your Cerebral Palsy is not heredity however, about three births out of ten thousand results in Cerebral Palsy…" unquote. This was tremendous good news.

One morning early in 1990, Eugenia said, "I think I'm pregnant." My thought was, "oh my goodness," and told her, "You better go to the doctor and be sure."

Over my adult years I have thought about being a dad and this was scary too. Eugenia confirmed she was pregnant and her face was radiant with joy and happiness.

Myself, I was happy also, but my concern was, I wanted our baby to be healthy and not disabled. Everyone was happy learning that Eugenia was pregnant, especially mom.

The big disappointment and sadness for me, dad passed before Eugenia became pregnant. And Eugenia's father passed before he seen Alexis.

Many times dad said, "Hurry up son, get busy, where is my grandchild." Surely, Dad and Alexis would have had a great grandpa and grandchild relationship. He loved children. He would have provided everything for Alexis.

We tied a pink ribbon onto the swing frame. And I just sat in the old manual wheelchair that I only used while taking long walks, usually shopping.

There I set about three feet away facing Alexis while pulling on the ribbon, swinging Alexis for hours whether she was awake or sleeping. This was a great joy.

Alexis and dad had similar mannerisms, even though their lives were decades apart. Such as picking up objects up off the floor with their toes, this I could only imagine doing.

Picking up and carrying Alexis around was impossible. Certainly did not want a government agency interfering with me as a disabled dad in raising my daughter, I wanted to be the best dad that I could be.

Alexis and just worked with each other, she crawled toward me, pulling herself into a standing position near me. We grabbed onto each other's clothing and worked together as she climbed up onto my lap.

After watching Alexis' first unassisted step without falling down, I knew Alexis would be alright, not disabled, oh a tremendous blessing. Alexis would stand in front of me and we would walk together as she held onto my crutches, as if were walking hand in hand together.

Some friends babysit Alexis while Eugenia worked in the pharmacy. Eugenia was happy being a mother, even with her responsibilities of helping me.

Eugenia worked full time, maintaining a household and every day's responsibilities. Everything fit nicely with Alexis being around our Christian friends' homes. Alexis was always in a good, safe, Christian babysitters, the Lord just blessed us again.

One afternoon I lost my balance and broke my neck, crashing headfirst into the bathroom wall. Alexis was three and one half years old. Eugenia came home from work with Alexis about five hours later and they found me on the bathroom floor.

While the emergency response people were assisting me in the bathroom, quietly,

Alexis was anxiously watching everything while leaning back against the hallway wall, squatting down on her heels.

As I was wheeled past her on the stretcher, I said to Alexis something like, "Alexis, daddy is going to the hospital but do not worry I will be okay."

Alexis looked worried and probably scared that her daddy was hurt, but how do you explain and reassure to a three year old, in a matter of two seconds, not to worry.

Oh what a brave little girl she was during those moments. She was quiet, never got in the way and never fussed. We know in her heart and mind that Alexis somehow just wanted to help her daddy.

But she did not know how, I was so proud of her. She was being brave, and yet very quiet. And I was deeply concerned over her thoughts and feelings in this troubling situation that Alexis is witnessing before her eyes.

It was impossible for a three year old to comprehend the implications of my fall and neck fracture, nobody could. It certainly was tough a time to remain strong because I did not know how or if I would recover and be a positive, helpful father for Alexis.

Depression set in quickly but I had to be strong and not show my fears so Alexis would remain a happy young child.

But I was so thankful that I was not wearing a halo brace. Within our group conversation, I remember Barry encouraging me when he said bluntly, "You need to suck it up."

During the period after my broken neck, there were not many good feeling about myself other than I still had Eugenia and Alexis in my life. My injury caused partial numbness and tingling in my hands and fingers was the most difficult and annoying psychological pain.

My spinal cord injury C-6 just added to the psychological problems of being in a body that I hated even worse and no longer understood.

One moment, Alexis came running toward me from observing the surroundings from a three and a half year's old point of view.

As Eugenia gently lifted Alexis up onto my lap and Eugenia softly reminded

Alexis, "Be careful with daddy's neck and don't squeeze his neck."

As Alexis and I looked into each other's eyes about six inches apart. But I started crying while Alexis and I held each other I could not help it.

During these times of struggle, I always wanted to be the best dad that I could be for Alexis, especially in communications.

On one occasion Alexis spoke up and said, "Daddy you are not listening to me." And I took her statement very seriously. Never do I want Alexis to feel "unheard."

During Alexi's infancy I could not be of much help in taking care her. But one of my activities would be swinging her in an infant swing. We tied a pink ribbon onto the swing frame. And I pulled on the ribbon as she st two feet in front of me as I sat in my manual wheelchair while in the house.

Some activities I never could do as a child, such as set up in bed unassisted, hold my head up or not having the abilities to stop drooling or grasp objects.

The best place for Alexis and I do our bonding was either when I laid in bed or when we were setting at the dining table.

Alexis was always eager to do things for me. Before the age of two, she was picking things up that I dropped such as an ink pen, a baseball cap. And putting things back into my hands or within my reach.

When Alexi's friend visited us, often I asked her to do things for me and Alexis would get jealous and tell her, "He is my daddy, I will help him."

Alexis learned from a very early age, to not rush in leaving my side, until all of the objects were placed securely within my grasp because I could easily drop them.

The "terrible two's," was not a problem for us. Eugenia would explain to Alexis that we did not have the money to purchase some things that Alexis ask for. There was no crying, fussing or any other negative behavior from Alexis.

Alexis' behavior and attitude seemed amazing to us. My mother thought otherwise, that we were spoiling Alexis.

When Alexis outgrew her clothes and toys she learned to share. And we shipped her clothes and other things to her Niece and other children, in the Philippines.

The summer of 1992, the three of us flew home to the Philippines. This was exciting to visit our family for the first time. Alexis was nineteen months old. We were not sure how Alexis would cope on the two day flight back home, so we purchased three airplane tickets to assure us as much comfortable space as possible.

In the Philippines many family members took care of Alexis. Family and friends brought over their young children to play with her, "the Princess of Amaya", people called Alexis.

It was troubling watching Alexis struggling with her life, I can only imagine how my parents felt with my struggles.

If Alexis listened to my guidance I believed I could teach Alexis to do things through faith and trust that I physically was incapable of doing. But I did my best to explain things, such as throwing and catching a softball, swinging a bat and riding a bicycle.

My stiff spastic legs could not pedal a bicycle and I had no sense of balance. Most parents would run along beside their children holding onto the bicycle but I could not do that.

Alexis and I at the top of our driveway which sloped down toward the street. She was on her bike and I sat near her in the wheelchair explaining how she needed to position her pedals.

Courageously, Alexis took off by herself on her bicycle, "Keep pedaling and watch for the cars," I hollered as she rolled down our old blacktop driveway. But near the mailbox Alexis tipped over and fell down, I cringed concerned about Alexi's safety.

Alexis jumped up and checked her hands, while adjusting her knee pads and helmet, and she yelled, "Daddy, when are you going to buy me a new bike, this stupid bike is not working?"

Like most parents I wanted to jump up and rush down the driveway to pick her up and check on Alexis. But I could not and I felt bad inside.

"The bike is not stupid Alexis. You need to get up, get back on and keep on going. Keep trying", I assured her. Then mom's quote came to my mind, one that I heard many times daily for years, "Can't never did anything. Try again."

"Come back up here and try again" I hollered and encouraged Alexis while motioning with my hand, to come back at the top of the driveway. My main goal was to teach Alexis, to keep trying new things until she succeeded.

After a few trips down the driveway Alexis gained confidence and she enjoyed riding her bicycle. And I was following her in my wheelchair as she quickly sped away ahead of me down the street.

We were doing the best we could without the help from family members. They lived in other states or overseas. Eugenia was filling in for me as a "father's role" in the things that I could not do, such as picking up and carrying Alexis.

Numerous other tasks, was added onto Eugenia's responsibilities that she had to do for each of us.

Alexis enjoyed "walking" with me as a toddler, as she stood in front of me holding onto the crutches, then we would just "walk," or in my case jostle, slowly through the house. Thank God we never fell down together.

And Alexis misspelled four spelling words during the third grade but I was disappointed in myself that Alexis missed four words because I should have made sure Alexis knew her words. She learned so quickly and easily, unlike me.

In the fourth grade, Alexis learned her multiplication tables riding on my wheelchair footrest throughout the house. She learned the whole multiplication tables by listening to me and then she would repeat them back to me in one afternoon. Mother drilled me for hours nightly and while waiting for the school bus.

Alexis had this unusual act of picking objects up off the floor with her toes, just like my dad had. That was interesting because dad had passed about twenty three months before Alexis was born.

How effortlessly that looked to me, putting on my own shoes and socks would have been a breeze. And I would have not been so embarrassed, in asking people to tie my shoes or hearing the phrase, "tie my shoes."

Alexis received several awards in school. She was selected to be a United States
Student Ambassador and she visited Australia and New Zealand in the seventh grade. In my seventh grade I barely passed.

As a freshman in high school Alexis was a member of the Forensic Class. The Forensic class students needed to select their own personal speech topic. And in writing their speeches they learned to develop the skills in formal speaking and compete with other students from other schools.

Alexis decided her speech topic would be on the two airplanes that crashed into the two World Trade Center Buildings, in New York City on September, 11, 2001. We worked on writing her speech and it was a joy.

She was doing things that seemed so easily for her but I could not do because of my Cerebral Palsy speech. Alexis competed with other contestants, some had four years of forensic speaking experience.

At that event, she placed ninth in the county competition. Oh I was so proud and happy for her to have the skills of public speaking, something that I always wished that I could do, be a better, understandable public speaker.

There were over six hundred students in her senior class Alexis was number three. In my senior class there were one hundred and six students my ranking was in the eighties range.

Alexis later earned a degree in nursing assistant in her two year course, her final grade was something like ninety seven percent oh, I was so proud of her. She had very similar results with other courses including her paralegal online course. It seemed like everything came so easily and quickly for Alexis.

Alexis was never afraid to try new things, which was good. One needs that determination to be successful, which is how Eugenia and I tried to raise Alexis.

We never did realize our dreams of raising Alexis in the Philippines. It would have been tremendous having Eugenia's family support structure. Alexis would have had more positive influential friends and extended family for support in the Philippines.

Sometimes, it was a bit sad because I wanted to have more playful, interactions with Alexis and to help her more. But I believe she understood our circumstances. And I believe over the years Alexis will continue on her path to her dreams.

We are blessed with two healthy, wonderful grandsons, Ashton and Ace. Our grandson's, has certainly brightened and enriched our lives as only grandchildren can. It is our tremendous blessings when "the Triple A's," come to visit us.

Ashton and Ace both ride around the house on my wheelchair, just as Alexis did. The boys understood at a young age that Grandpa Shipe is a little different. Eugenia will teach them Tagalog. Our grandson's call me, "Wo Wo" a Filipino word meaning grandpa. And "Wa Wa" for grandma.

When Ashton was two, he picked up a small cracker crumb from my lap. With his out stretched arms he still could not reach my mouth, to feed me that broken cracker crumb, as I set in my wheelchair.

Then Ashton tossed the cracker crumb at me, with the hope of feeding me the cracker crumb. After a few attempts Ashton's missed my mouth again, but that was alright. He did his best and thought of other alternatives.

Ashton did not give in, he did not quit. Finally, he handed me the cracker. Certainly I will keep that moment in my life forever, I was quite proud of him. Now Ashton steps up on my wheelchair footrests and stands on my feet to be closer with me and we have a great time.

As time goes on, both Ashton and Ace will be very helpful to me. They will understand at a very early age that great success and good things can happen, even when plans need to be changed.

Occasionally, Ashton positioning his right hand, as I often hold my right hand into a fist position. And he knows when we do our high five hand slapping we do it with our left hands because my left hand opens up more normally than my right hand. He has some great athletic skills already at the age of four. And you can be assured that Ace, is watching everything.

My grandchildren already understand our special situation. When our children and grandchildren come to visit us for no particular reason, it just makes our day and brings us love, joy and happiness as "the Triple A's", Alexis, Ashton and Ace, brings to us. Praise the Lord.

Someday my grandchildren will learn from my writings to do their very best. When they see someone in a wheelchair, surely they will think of me and maybe be helpful to the wheelchair person also.

It is my prayers, with my writings and dreams that my grandchildren will do their very best in life, and to be helpful to others, sometime along their life journeys.

But most of all I pray, for grandchildren's health, safety and to believe in Jesus Christ and a place called Heaven. When my time comes to be with Lord Jesus Christ, everyone can look up at the stars. Then think of the stars as spotlights shining on themselves, so I can see them from Heaven. And know that I love my family for eternal life.

Our life long family friend Sharon also commented, "You have waited a long time to run down that basketball court and shoot the winning shot. Sounds great but your work here is not over. Keep up your encouraging and enlightening of the rest of us, Lon." Unquote.

And some starry night, I will tell Ashton and Ace and future grandchildren, "Just look up at stars and believe that starry light is God's way of me looking down at them from Heaven. And I love them very much."

Our Philippine Visits

It September 2002, we visited the Philippines for the first time to visit Eugenia's family and friends. For Eugenia it was a major life changing decision to leave her country, friends and family. Eugenia did fly here with the intentions of marrying me, a disabled person. Certainly a tremendous responsibility, on top of starting her new life in the United States.

One evening soon after we were married, Eugenia, was crying on the bathroom floor. She was home sick and missed her family, friends, culture and cuisine.

Communicating overseas was difficult, her family nor we had the Internet or telephone to communicate with her family for a few years, and I felt sad for her.

Eugenia was here for nearly three months before we were married on December 10, 1983. After we married, Eugenia worked at the local fast food restaurant. There she met a local customer Walter and his wife is a Filipina. Eugenia was so excited in learning there were many Filipinos in the local neighborhood.

Meeting the local Filipina in the neighborhood helped with Eugenia's recovery from her homesickness. They both spoke Tagalog, eat their cuisine and introduced us to other local Filipinos. We became members of the local Filipino Club.

Alexis our daughter, was thirty-four months old when we visited the Philippines. The Filipina Stewardesses were very helpful with Alexis.

The airline personnel wheeled me down the aisle in an aisle cart. Then two men physically transferred my airplane seat. Eugenia kept her eye on Alexis, giving instructions to the men helping me, and carrying our carryon luggage. Once seated a Stewardess pinned an Airlines Wings on Alexis dress and she was very happy. Alexis never caused any fuss during the twenty-some hour flight.

Once I am seated in an airplane, I sat there for the duration of my flight. We learned to be discreet and improvise with blankets, my hand held plastic urinal, adult depends, and not much fluid intake the day before and during the flight.

Eugenia stood in line for the airplanes restroom to empty my urinal, which was covered by a sweater in her hand. This is a embarrassing for us but it worked well. Usually when flying the three of us, are the first three passengers on the airplane and the last ones off.

Eugenia's family picked us up at the Manila airport with another hour drive we arrived in Cavite City at my brother-in-laws or "Kuya's" House. "Kuya" is a name the Filipinos use to show respect for their male elders.

"Kuya" had a comfortable middle class home, with linoleum covering concrete floors in the living room and kitchen. The walls were paneled or painted nicely. The three small bedrooms were just bare concrete. The one story house had electricity, running water and indoor plumbing.

However our adult Nephew would retrieve water from a community water hand pump across the street with a pail for flushing the toilet, bathing, cooking, laundry etc to save money.

Kuya's home was filled with love and each family member did their household duties. Kuya and "Ate" (pronounced as At a), worked seven days a week at the market, selling their goods in their family store, something like a flea market booth in the United States, a good middle class income.

Upon arriving late at night our niece was sound asleep on the living room floor. She gave up her bedroom for me to use. Her bed had the only mattress in the house. And most likely, the mattress was just recently purchased for me to use.

Throughout the days and evenings friends came to visit us. Sometimes children would be outside waiting to play with Alexis, the first American they ever seen.

The South Eastern China sea was a two minute walk away and the breeze smelled refreshing pleasant. The tropical heat was tolerable in a shaded area.

The next day we visited Eugenia's mother's house in Amaya, a barrio one could walk in fifteen minutes. Upon arriving Eugenia spoke up from the back of the private jeepney and said, "Welcome to our mansion."

Several people excitedly rushed out of the house to greet and help us unload our luggage and boxes. Then I see my elderly mother in law walked slowly out the front door to greet us, with her long dress and walking stick.

The two story wooden frame house certainly needed painting from the faded green color. Suddenly, the meaning of "culture shock" over whelmed me with the bare cement floors. The plywood windows with no glass or window screens swung outward to open.

But Jesus kept my heart and mind open with these unusual and exciting cultural events and situations. Certainly, I expected living conditions to be different but it was still a culture shock in the small house with bare, gray cement blocks with uneven or missing mortar between the blocks.

The bottom floor of the house might have been about the size of a one car garage in the United States, with the bedrooms upstairs. Within minutes, we were setting in Julius's house, my youngest brother in law.

Now there was dozens of people standing outside smiling, talking, looking waiting to greet us. Some people peaked through the open wooden shutters that had no glass or screens.

Suddenly everything became very comfortable for me. The joy and comforting of every family member and friends were tremendous.

My brother in law offered me their wedding gift, a set of unused silver wear to eat with. But I explained to him and Eugenia, what everyone used was fine with me. Certainly, I did not want to be treated like I was special or rich but just family. Many Filipinos eat with their hands but all I needed was a glass, plate and silverware.

My attitude helped my in-law feel more comfortable with me being in his house. Some Filipinos think all American's are rich because we have houses and automobiles.

When my male family members and friends were shirtless, I was shirtless, I just wanted to be a part of their culture, like them, a Filipino.

Eugenia is a fabulous cook, but I will not eat "blood pudding or balute fetus inside of an egg. Our niece was teasing, giggling and trying to convince me that balute was good for me, to keep my body strong. Blood pudding, the name just sounds nasty. Balute and blood pudding, I could not look at, yet alone eat.

English is taught in the Philippines schools as a secondary language. The younger generations speak much better English as Eugenia does. Ni, my mother-in-law and I got along really well, although she did not speak English. So others would translate for us, I could tell she was a fun loving person.

Often Ni, and I just set and look at each other and start giggling. Ni spoke to me in Tagalog, as if I knew every word she was saying, yet she knew I could not speak Tagalog.

Eugenia and I paid for everything, The US dollar exchange rate was one to twenty four pesos. The monthly electric bill might only be, in United States currency – four dollars.

They did not have a heating, air conditioning, water, cablevision or a sewer bill. Their basic bills were electricity, food and public transportation. Their water came from the hand water pump, just outside the back door. Millions of Filipinos lived on meager wages less than fifty dollars a month.

If a foreigner had a steady, monthly income of around one thousand dollars in 1992 they could live very comfortably in the Philippines.

The three of us slept in the living room couch which folded down into a large bed. Our oldest nephew, maybe in his mid-twenties on our first visit to the Philippines. He and Eugenia were my main caretakers.

He helped my life to be more enjoyable and comfortable in every way. Every night, our nephew folded the living room couch into our bed into the proper position and hung the mosquito net above our bed.

After sunset, the mosquito's came out very heavily. But I never understood why very few mosquito's came inside the house even though the doors and windows were open.

One evening, while sleeping on my right side, with Eugenia sleeping directly behind my back. Suddenly, I felt something brush against my right elbow.

Immediately, I thought, it had to be a rat, I heard stories how the rats would eat the garbage at night. Scared to death on being bitten, I elbowed Eugenia and yelled, "Eugene, there is something in our bed." Quickly she sat up in bed, in the dark living room and she began pawing through the bed cover.

"I can't find anything," she said sleepily.

"Turn on the light," I loudly whispered to her, "So you can see." Eugenia scrambled out of bed, flipped on the single hanging bare ceiling light bulb on. As she searched through the mosquito netting that hung above and around the bed.

We see a rat tangled up in the mosquito net searching for an escape route. Eugenia quickly tugged on the mosquito net and the rat was gone in a flash. Certainly, I did not sleep after that.

The next morning everyone learned about the rat that was in our bed. Mother mentioned while laughing and speaking Tagalog, in her toothless mouth, "Maybe that was your Father in Law trying to see who was in the house," Eugenia translated to me.

"Well, I hope the rat never comes back," I uneasily said to everyone in the room. Ni wanted to know how big the rat was, so I set my hands about four inches apart to demonstrate how long the rat, might have been.

Soon dozens of people heard about the rat story that was in my bed. Each time I showed everyone how big the rat was with my hands, it grew a bit longer. But by now, the rat was about two feet long, and Ni would always laugh louder and say something to me in Tagalog.

With her hand signals she compared the rat size to other male human anatomy parts, I understood what she was saying.

Many things opened my eyes, on the culture shock. Some I expected, until you see the differences in the cultures, it is beyond the imagination. You may see the history, the beauty. Then look in another direction and you may see the poverty and pollution.

Observing the living conditions, the children begging on the streets in Manila, that was a very uneasy feeling for me. Our jeepney or van drivers were family friends.

A jeepney had long benches on both sides of the back half of the passenger section. With a metal roof to keep the sun or rain from everyone. Usually I set up in the front seat with the driver and our nephew.

He helped me in everything, such as pushing me around in my manual or wheelchair and assisted in every physical transfer or activity that needed to be done.

My favorite place was Amaya. Cavite City was a larger city with more traffic. While setting on the street corners in my wheelchair, I enjoyed watching the colorful jeepneys whiz by, or watch the street vendor's peddle their goods to customers along the way.

Amaya had a slower pace of living and many street vendors would walk the cement street. The vendors all knew Eugenia's family well. And the vendors sold everything that you might need for the day, at your front door, for pennies a day, if you had United States dollars.

Many street vendors and friends would stop in my mother in laws house to greet and visit her. Then learn about me because I was an American, maybe some people never seen an American before.

Sometimes the vendors were shy and did not speak English but they interacted with Eugenia. She was always around in the morning to help get me up and going in my wheelchair along with our nephew's help.

Daily, I enjoyed setting in the wheelchair under the covered patio watching the villagers walk past the house about fifteen feet from the street. My brother in law built houses, made furniture and cabinet on the patio, which I enjoyed watching. Visitors was a steady stream from morning until late evening, I loved that too and everyone who visited.

One afternoon, while I sat on the patio, five girls, maybe they were in the fifth grade approached me shyly and giggling. The girls stood in a semi-circle in front me. Some were smiling and one or two were speaking Tagalog. Finally, as I set there smiling, one of the girls spoke up and she asked me, "What is your name?" I happily answered her,

Then I asked the girls in English "how are you in English?" And the girl who spoke to me earlier replied by saying, "Fine." The same girl and I chatted for less than a minute and I realized she struggled speaking English but she had great courage.

Then in a flash, the girls turned and ran down the street, yelling and giggling. Those five girls gave me a thought. It would be a blessing to teach English to some of the children or adults.

We made four visits to the Philippines since June of 1992. During our second trip to the Philippines Eugenia and I wanted to repair and remodel brother and sister in laws houses.

Those two houses approximately one thousand square meters together needed major repair on the cement floors. My brother in law and his friends did the labor for maybe ten dollars a day.

They added a new room connecting the two houses approximately one hundred twenty square feet from the foundation, floor to the roof.

Julius house has three small bedrooms upstairs, but I never went upstairs. The bedroom windows were made of wood that glided sideways alone the outside walls.

Over the years, before we built the front patio, people tracked in mud through the main path way on the rough gray cement flooring, from the front door to the back door had a much darker brown color.

Our total construction costs with labor and materials was less than two thousand U.S. Dollars.

Many houses were made of bamboo, or had rough concrete with mud caked flooring or simply had dirt floors. Every baby, infant or toddler was carried everywhere by family or nannies, until they were walking with flip-flops. So babies learned to crawl while they were on the furniture and or the beds.

My brother in law is well known throughout the area for his amazing, expert carpenter, in making furniture and cabinets maker. One carpenter/concrete skills I observed watching Julius was new to me. The Filipinos shifted their own sand and concrete mix by a wire screen and a wooden frame with four wooden handles.

Once the shifting was complete they added water to the sand and cement mix right on the porch and mixed everything together with shovels, making their own cement. In the United States we have cement trucks, power tools and other tools for our various construction needs.

It was interesting to watch how the construction techniques were different between the United States and the Philippines.

My sister in laws house, needed much more major construction and repair. Her house was partially made of cement hollow block, plywood and bamboo. Her house had a partial cement floor that had cracked and shifted to the point where there was a three or four inch difference in height in her house flooring.

The other part of her house, nipa hut had a dirt floor. On the outside front door area on her house was small wooden frame patrician covered with bamboo material to keep the wind and rain from blowing onto her plywood front door.

Caloy also helped with the construction projects, grabbed the edge of the patrician with his hands and he shook the whole patrician and it crashed onto the ground in a heap, with dust flying all around and on his sweaty, shirtless back.

We noticed my sister in law was excited but sad with the home improvements, she was almost in tears. From sadness, I think in watching a large part of her house wall demolished within a matter of seconds. The house was nearly the size of a one car-garage in the United States.

Within a few days the men poured the concrete flooring, added a small hollow block living room from the ground up, with windows, two doors, electricity and roofing that connected my sister in laws house to "Ni's house."

It was truly a joy and a blessing to repair her house, add on a new room, new concrete flooring, all for around two thousand United States dollars.

She struggled and worked hard all her life raising three children`. Her only income was washing clothes by hand, eight or more hours daily, and maybe seven days a week, in her barrio for maybe a dollar a day, if she could find work.

Other people we enjoyed helping, such as Arman and we became good friends too. Armando might have been in his forties, married with two children. He was a very skilled construction worker, and nobody could out work him. He would never turn down work Julius told me one time. His wages was about one dollar a day. Arman often help Julius, on construction jobs. He always had a jolly attitude with a big top front toothless smile.

My wife and I are only two people and we try to help as many people in the Philippines as we can, a shirt to this person, a pair of flip flop slippers to another person or a can of soup to another person.

Throughout the year we ship a few balik-bayan boxes to the Philippines. This is a joy for us to help as many people as possible. Truly, it is not always easy to help others in the Philippines, when we have our own living expenses. My wife, Eugenia works very hard Pharmacist Technician. We do our best to help our Filipino friends and family.

The pollution, littering, slums, street people, crime the beggars are everywhere. We need to look at things as individuals, 'How can we help someone, somewhere sometime, somehow?''

When we look at the good we can do the simplest things to help one another. One of my dreams if we retire in the Philippines, is financing a student's college education, this is possible with a few hundred dollars a year.

A monthly home health care aid working forty hours a week, in the Philippines, would be cheaper than our electric bill in the states. In the Philippines, family takes care of family. There I would not need to sign over our assets to the nursing home, like we do in the states. And Eugenia would have more support in taking care of me.

The morning we were returning home to the United States after our two month visit in 1998, was very difficult for me, certainly I did not want to go home, I loved and wanted to stay in the Philippines.

While our family was loading the luggage in the van, I started crying. Eugenia asked, "Do you want to stay here in the Philippines?" I shook my head "no" with the tears rolling down my face.

My wife and daughter were going home and my heart said, I needed to go home with them. If my family left without me, I would have regretted immediately not going with them.

But my heart is in Amaya with my Filipino family as the jeepney slowly weaved through the narrow streets in Amaya. And I waved at everyone, several hundred people, friends, family and neighbors all lined the streets for several blocks.

They were shouting and waving, as we slowly drove past them. Still crying like a child, I did not want to leave these great people. For nearly an hour, until we reached the airport, I cried.

Yes, I want to go home to the Philippines but how can I leave my daughter and two grandsons here in the States. Maybe, they could visit us there.

My University

My life at my senior college, now a University, was an awesome experience. But there is too much to say in this book, with numerous great memories, along with the difficult times. Many names I do not remember, but their kindness and helpfulness will never be forgotten.

Certainly, I met many amazing people who just accepted me for who I wanted to be, a student and friend, "you were just one of the guys," my good friend Terry told me one evening and that is all I wanted to be, one of the guys and a good student.

College was not easy, good grades was still a struggle. The awards from "Who's Who In American Junior Colleges in 1973 and Phi Sigma Tau National Honor Society in Philosophy was a very proud moment for me.

And going through a couple of years of "not liking myself" or depression. What brought me through to my undergraduate and Graduate School programs, were my colleagues, my friends.

My friends carried my lunch trays, book satchel and the guys from "Kappa House" carried me up and down the stairs so I could get to class, and up four floors to hang out and party with everyone.

The guys who lived in my dorm in "Moose Hall" came busting into my dorm room, rushing to get me dress in a matter of seconds during the fire alarms. Many fire alarms were maliciously set off by students, as many as three a night. Then we stood in the freezing snow outside until we had permission to re-enter the buildings.

And the "Moose Hall" guys would walk past my dorm room, when the door would be open and say to me, "Tie my shoes."

With these "Moose Hall" guys the phrase, "Tie My Shoes" came alive because they always tied my shoes. Dino and his sister, as well as many other friends brought in my clothes from my car to my dorm room or out to my car to go home, which was on the main floor.

My dorm door was always open and students and friends were always dropping in to visit me and talk. Names and many conversations have since been forgotten, but the dorm experiences and faces are still in my heart today.

College physically and emotionally would have been impossible for me to continue on. Several dozens of people helped me make it through my daily college years, "thank you each and every one of you for everything."

My professors were amazing, they helped me in every way they could, when I did not understand things.

My international friends were fantastic, I enjoyed being around them and learning about their countries and cultures.

For there to be an ending to my college years that began on September 1971 at my junior college and completed after Graduate School at my Catholic University in August 1982, there is no ending to the memories. Perhaps those memories will be in another future book.

In Closing

In 1972, I shared my thoughts on writing my story with my English Professors Ron and Tom who at my junior college and now about forty-six years later, this journey has been painful and rough going in life and in writing my story.

On the other hand, my life has been truly blessed and I have accomplished things and experienced life's blessings beyond my imagination.

The people in my life, especially my family and most importantly my Lord Jesus Christ who was with me in every breath of my life.

The purpose for writing this journey is not for my fame or glory but to help someone to keep going and striving for their best.

We may need to change our plans but we must never give up on ourselves. Always do your best, because someone is always watching and rooting for your successes and dreams to come true.

Here is my winning touchdown, winning free throw and walk off home run Terry and Larry, my story, I hope you and everyone enjoys reading it.

While living in the dorm at college, I asked my college buddies to, tie my shoes please. Soon they would shout as they passed my dorm room, "Tie My Shoes."

Sometime, I will never need to say, "Tie My Shoes" but in Heaven, I will walk, run and then dance.

Lonnie E. Shipe

FAMILY PHOTO

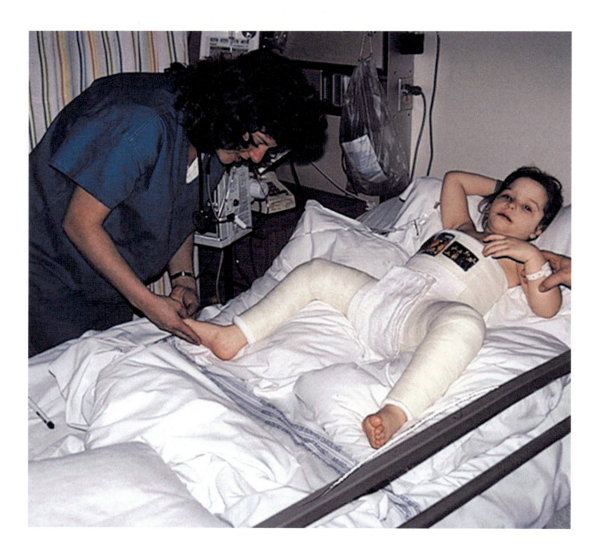

picture of a body cast from my chest to toes

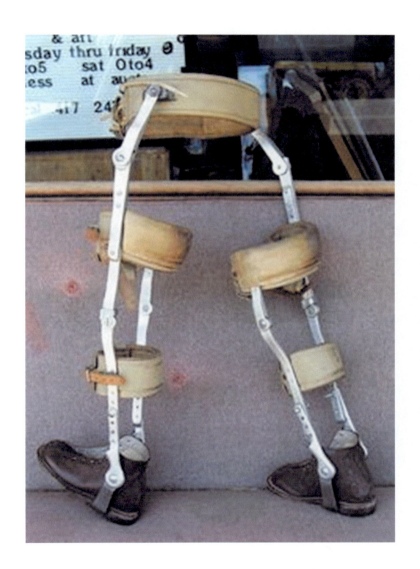

knee-brace-braces

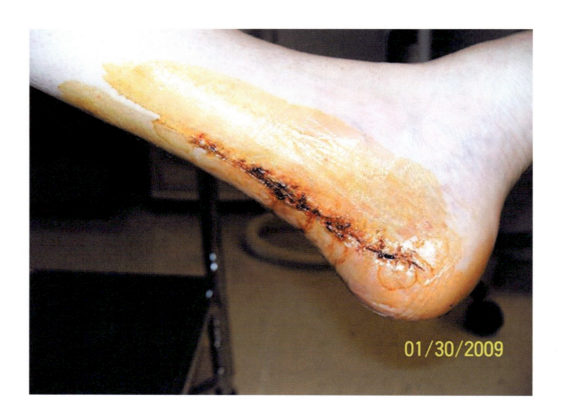

01/30/2009

Surgery on my Achillies tendons on both legs

grandson's AShton (front), Eugenia holding Ace, Lonnie

wife Eugenia and mE

garden tractor

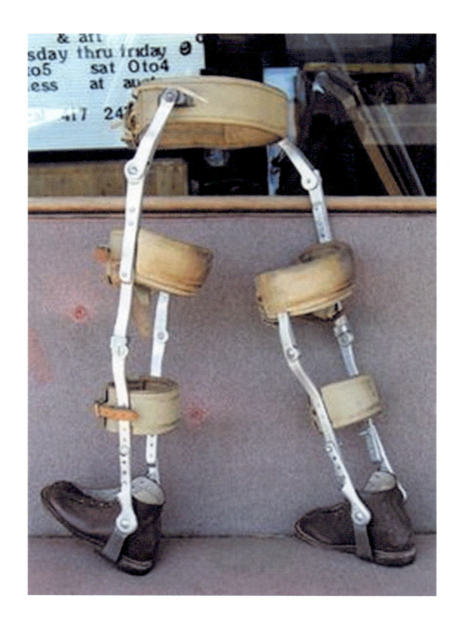

knee-brace-braces

Printed in the United States
By Bookmasters